Professional Warrior

The Everyday Summit

Tim Krause, PhD

Karolee Krause, LPC, SAC

About the Authors

Tim Krause has worked with and in a number of Fortune 100 companies in the fields of higher education, finance, healthcare, technology, and food and food ingredients. He works with business leaders in understanding and leading their organizations through change and uncertainty.

Tim currently teaches University-level courses focused on the development of interpersonal skills, decision-making, and change management at the undergraduate and graduate levels. He has pioneered a number of approaches to teaching communication that rely on role playing, simulation and case studies to help leaders develop the skills they need in a world that moves at unforgiving and break-neck speed.

Karolee Krause is a clinical consultant, Licensed Professional Counselor (LPC), Substance Abuse Counselor (SAC), and author with extensive experience in the areas of leadership, personal development, health and wellness, and addictions and recovery.

Karolee is passionate about creating positive change in the areas of authentic leadership, personal and professional success, career coaching, stress management, and life transitions.

Whether through program development, team building or professional coaching, Karolee's goal is to foster, motivate, and inspire personal and professional success.

Table of Contents

Introduction 9
Preface 17
Preparing Your Way 25
    Obstacles 28
    Office Floors 30
    Tools and Rewards 31
    Tools for the Journey 34
    Mission 36
    Preparation 37
    Rejuvenation 41
    The Unpredictable 44
The Way of the Warrior 51
A Humble Beginning 57
Phase 1: Commitment to Change 63
Phase 2: A Path of Transformation 95
Phase 3: Navigating Treacherous Water 123
Phase 4: Professional Darkness 159
Phase 5: Climbing Higher 199
Phase 6: Crucial Decisions 231
Phase 7: The Professional Warrior's Summit 269
The Professional Pinnacle 287
Appendices 305

Introduction

Professional Warrior: The Everyday Summit was written as a motivational self-help guide and personal success book in which you will take the journey of your lifetime, to become a leader and warrior within.

You are about to embark on one of the most rewarding and challenging adventures you have ever taken. Throughout the journey, you will discover personal and professional strengths and skills you did not know you had. You will find unexpected messages and learn to follow your own intuitive guidance to empower and help you get to the next level in your career, and ultimately to the summit of your own professional ladder of success.

In *Professional Warrior: The Everyday Summit*, you will learn to climb over enormous professional blockages, hike up steep staircases of stress management, conquer employee conflicts, walk across fire pits of angry customers or clients, swim across the sea of diversity, and crawl through dark cut-throat hallways of competition. The adventure is not for the weak of mind, spirit, or body, but for those with the bravery to accept the challenge to reach the summit.

As a warrior, your journey is one in which you will commit to a new path, one of personal strength and power that will ultimately lead you to become the best leader for yourself and to those you lead.

Learn to leave behind old, maladaptive personal and professional patterns, and destructive business decisions, as you gain mastery over your own leadership style and skills.

Keep in mind, though, that climbing to the top won't be without its struggles. As in daily life, we all face personal and professional difficulties, as well as nearly impossible choices and decisions. The difference between you and others around you is that as a leader, you know that when you reach the summit of your career, you will never want to return to life as you once knew it because you will have learned to face difficult business decisions with fairness, integrity, and honesty. You will have succeeded, not by stepping over others, but by simply being the best leader and warrior within.

Part of your journey will involve using personal and professional tools that you will gather on your adventure. You will use them to overcome the challenges of everyday life.

Never forget that warriors are relentlessly tested as they commit to personal goals to reach the summit. Through emotional and mental strength, spiritual guidance, and physical endurance, the warrior finally reaches his or her true destination: the true self and becomes the ultimate leader that thrives as they learn to lead others in their own personal quests of professional success.

As you prepare for the journey of a lifetime, remember that becoming a warrior means releasing the past, facing unknown fears and uncertainties, saying goodbye to familiar people, and stepping onto an unknown and unfamiliar path. This is not an adventure for those who lack courage.

You will not be entirely alone on your ascent to the summit or top of the professional ladder because warriors are guided every step of the way, while they also recognize that their strongest guide is their own inner wisdom.

Life presents many pathways and so too will this journey. Every day there is an opportunity to step outside of repetitive and familiar patterns, unhealthy habits, and dead-end behaviors. A new path, the warrior's path is about to begin. If you are ready, this moment offers a new journey, one that will change your life forever.

Journey with other leaders in the climb for professional success as you learn to overcome common work-related issues in the areas of conflict resolution, emotional intelligence, team building, and employee grievances. Learn to incorporate stress management skills both personally and professionally as you continue your daily climb and learn how to avoid professional burnout and work-related stress.

Preface

Professional Warrior: The Everyday Summit is written to assist those of you who are in the process of making the decision to climb today's corporate ladder. The decision is a considerable one, requiring careful thought and consideration.

Along the way to the summit, the professional warrior faces all sorts of obstacles and challenges on his or her way to the top including political dilemmas, ethical decisions, the risk of pay cuts, added job responsibilities, corporate takeovers, and the stress associated with toxic employees and environments.

In *Professional Warrior*, we guide you through different types of business scenarios that will help lead you further to the summit. Be warned, however, that the way is fraught with danger and has the potential to drag you back down the ladder to a job that you may feel over-qualified for, or that you feel no longer serves you.

The way forward in your career requires care, however, because it is just as possible that your climb to the top could result in overwork, stress, physical depletion or unhappiness. Any of these pitfalls, may end with regret in making the climb. However, once you start your journey you will be faced with the decision to stay on that path or climb back down to a professional level with little or no prestige or recognition. Always remember that the destination, up or down the ladder, is less important than your conscious choices about your career path. You may ultimately be just as happy stepping back from the journey, even as you are in progressing forward.

Professional Warriors make difficult decisions on a daily basis. Their decisions not only affect themselves, but their entire team, and often family and friends. Those decisions, as well as intentional decisions to lead, will be based on personal and professional experience, knowledge and your own inner guidance.

Making the decision to climb to the top, or to stay in an entry level position is a personal choice that can bring great reward and recognition or it can bring even more significant pitfalls, poor health, or negatively affect personal and professional relationships.

Professional Warriors: The Everyday Summit will help you address a number of important questions as you begin your journey.

Are you climbing for the right reasons?

What will you gain at the top that you do not already have?

Will others support you on the climb or will they sabotage you, attempting to hinder your progress?

If you attain the height of your career, what more remains for you to accomplish?

Can you become a better leader or a professional warrior that others will respect and follow?

Climbing the ladder of success is not for the weak, but for those who have the motivation and drive to be the best warrior they can be. To achieve that level of success, this book focuses on the multiple dimensions of the decision-making process as well as the leadership skills required to be successful.

Professional Warrior: The Everyday Summit is written as a motivational and leadership success book to help you find the right professional path as you gain in the areas of emotional intelligence, personal empowerment, and leadership skills. It emphasizes a very personal approach to not only defining success, but to helping you find the right path that will facilitate your journey to the summit.

This book also provides you with different professional scenarios that you may endure or encounter along your way. It will help you identify and deal with the psychological, emotional, and intellectual aspects of why people climb, the experiences they have, and how this kind of journey helps or harms them emotionally or mentally along the way.

Professional Warrior: The Everyday Summit addresses professional and psychological challenges faced when making the climb to the top and provides tools for those who climb. At the end of your journey, you will have developed the skills necessary for your own personal success only to discover that the final destination truly rests with each and every one of us.

Preparing Your Way

Throughout your journey to the summit you will be offered several survival tools and specific guidance every step of the way. Your mission will be to find, collect and apply essential leadership tools to your own unique circumstances. To those who seek them out, you will find messages that are hidden in the office building to help you stay on the warrior's path and ultimately reach the summit of your profession.

The obstacles and challenges that you will encounter as a warrior, along with the tools, skills, and techniques that you will find throughout the journey are described in this section.

Obstacles

The path to the summit or executive suite might appear easy at first but it will quickly change and become steeper and more difficult to climb as you strive to attain the top.

Over the course of your career, you will work through professional blockages, hike up steep staircases of stress management as you work excessively long hours, conquer employee conflicts complex and fraught with danger, walk across fire pits of angry customers or navigate challenging clients to satisfy their every need. You will swim across the sea of diversity to keep your team in an appropriate balance that will assist them as they excel in their work. With your team at your side, you will crawl through cut-throat hallways of competition as you compete with a myriad of others who seek and strive to reach the top, much like you. However, only the best warrior or leader will make the journey and succeed. How will you ensure that it is you?

At times, it will feel as though you are crawling through the dark, lonely hallways as you feel as though you are navigating the leadership role alone. However, turning back will no longer be an option, and you will not want to return to your old position, employer or profession. No matter how difficult the journey becomes, you renew an oath to yourself to move forward, up the corporate ladder and into a position of greater respect and responsibility as you learn to lead with a warrior's vision of fairness and integrity.

Office Floors

A length journey requiring significant courage, you will not ascend to the summit or executive suite easily or in one short day—or even a year. But you will not make the journey entirely alone, either. You will be aided as you progress through a series of offices and building floors where you will rest, restore your mind, and body as the journey provides you with ever greater challenges.

Office floors, however, are never permanent, and you will not stay on any one of them for very long as you force yourself to continue in your relentless quest to the top.

Tools and Rewards

In our professional lives, we are often given the impression that leaders somehow possess natural or innate abilities. It is the belief that some of us are born leaders, and others are not. In our experience, nothing could be further from the truth. Leadership skills can and should be cultivated- a process you will discover that requires a variety of tools, relationships and sets of circumstances.

The challenge that you will discover in this journey is that professional tools are often hidden from view in a variety of locations throughout your journey. While these items will give you strength and endurance to help you get to the next floor and ultimately to your final destination, they are often not immediately evident either. It is no accident that the resources that you need to be successful are typically hidden from view: their very existence challenge the narrative or story that leaders are born naturally, and not developed. This reality means that you will have to actively seek out the tools that you need to be successful in your leadership roles. If you are fortunate, and learn to ask the right questions of the right people, your colleagues, peers and supervisor will help you identify those resources.

In addition to those very tangible resources, you will also discover intuitive messages, tools and guidance along your journey, but only if you look carefully and in the right places. Messages may be carved on desktops, sit on unused bookshelves, or appear subtly in the light that drifts through your office window. They may be encoded in a conversation that you have with a colleague over lunch. Intuitive guidance, and the ability to make connections that others do not see or hear, will encourage you to continue the warrior's journey and guide you every step of the way—but only if you are willing to seek it out.

Tools for the Journey

Emotional, mental, spiritual and physical self-care tools will be found on each floor along the way. These tools are not always easy to find, but once found, they will help you move up the ladder of success.

Not all of the tools that you will be offered will be useful to you but you should still consider them carefully as some of them may be more useful than they first appear. Remember that successful leaders are both willing and eager to step outside of their comfort zones when considering the tools and opportunities with which they are faced. With time and experience you will learn which tools are right for you, and which ones you might choose to set aside for another time, or for someone else. These are not always easy decisions and we will provide you with the resources to help you explore new opportunities and resources with your team, evaluate them, use them when they work, adapt them as necessary, or set them aside when they don't.

Mission

This is challenging and engaging work. It will be easy to get caught up in the day-to-day details of your efforts. However, never forget that your mission is to become the warrior leader that is respected, valued, and trusted as you rise above everyday professional problems, and overcome leadership pitfalls and professional burnout.

As you head down this path you will always want to remember your ultimate mission:

*I will become the **warrior leader** that is respected, valued and trusted.*

Preparation

Beginning in your modest office cubicle, you must take inventory of what you need to leave behind to begin your journey to the top, including toxic thinking patterns, self-doubt and any form of destructive energy that may keep you stuck in a negative professional cycle that prevents you from moving upward.

The warrior's path will be filled with slippery steps and destructive meetings, but what is more dangerous than the journey itself is fear, both paralyzing fear of success and fear of failure in not reaching the summit.

The warrior must abandon all fear of the journey because if she or he does not, the warrior will not succeed. Do not forget, however, that it is easier to say that you will let go of fear than it is to actually do it. One way to address that challenge is through thoughtful planning. A short series of questions at the end of each section of the book will not only help guide and prepare you for the journey that you face but should reinforce the fact that you are more prepared for this journey than you might realize. Sometimes the very act of planning helps us regain a sense of control and alleviate some of our greatest fears.

Fear and self-doubt will always return, usually at unexpected times, and when it is most inconvenient as the warrior's climb gains in elevation and status. The small act of acknowledging this reality is a paradox in that it results in the greater advantage of taking control of those self-doubts because we can control that which we acknowledge.

Remember too that sometimes our fears will seem paralyzing and will take many forms that we may not immediately recognize. Some of the more common fears that you will encounter include slipping and falling off the path, not being successful in your role and even fear of failure as a whole. With such an inward focus, it is easy to forget that some of those fears stem from outside forces that warriors also must conquer: the fear of failure that comes from the fear of letting down others.

The fear of disappointing our team, colleagues, supervisors, friends and family can be the most debilitating fears of all. Warriors remember, however, that fear often has its roots in the fear of lacking or losing control. In many cases, the strongest warriors not only understand what they control, but also learn to let go of those things which they cannot control.

What sets warriors apart is not that they don't feel fear or have self-doubts, but that they don't dwell on either of those types of thoughts. Warrior leaders learn to overcome their fears and as they do, they teach others to conquer their own fears as well.

Rejuvenation

Along your journey, you will discover three banners, each

located at key locations in your journey to the summit. The first of the banners will be found at the building entrance, the next at the half-way point in your journey, and the final banner hangs from the summit of the executive suite and board room. The three banners and their colors represent aspects of your journey. The first banner begins with the color green for marking your willingness to begin the journey. It represents new beginnings, growth, and self-care.

The second banner in your journey is red and is located around the mid-point. Halfway through your journey, you will find yourself in a transitional place where you must make the decision to continue to climb to the summit, a difficult and painful decision for many of us to make. Or you might make the decision to retreat back to the career or professional position you left behind. But if and when you make the choice to continue, you will have to fully commit to your journey to the summit.

The red flag represents power and danger, and the choices that you will make in the face of many obstacles in your journey. The real power at the mid-point rests with your choice to continue to the summit or return to a position you left behind in the past.

The final and ultimate banner in your journey is royal blue. This flag is located at the mountain's summit, the corporate suite and represents leadership, wisdom, strength and conquest. As you reach the end of your journey, you will be bestowed with wisdom and guidance as you continue your life as the professional warrior and move forward as a newfound leader.

The Unpredictable

Along your journey, you will need to search for time and places to rest and replenish your body, mind, and spirit. At times, that rest may appear as though it is a setback; remind yourself that journeys take many forms and alternate paths that as warriors we sometimes have to forge and make our own. Although you will often rely upon the office floors for respite from your arduous journey, you will also find wellness and meditation rooms along the way to rest in. At other times you may have to recognize that you will need to create your own space from the resources provided around you. As in life, you won't always have retreats or wellness rooms to go to and will have to create our own.

Finally, with resolve you are ready to begin your journey. You begin in a time and location that you choose to accept as your own.

You laugh quietly to yourself at the plain-sounding words in your head, but you take that first small step onward, and remind yourself of your ultimate destination:

*I will become the **warrior leader** that is respected, valued and trusted.*

Your Departure Checklist

1. Identify one behavior that you would like to leave behind as you begin your journey.

2. Describe one tangible step that you will take to change or abandon that behavior.

3. Consider the successes of those around you and identify one behavior that you would like to learn to emulate.

4. Identify one actionable way in which you will adapt that behavior and make it your own.

5. What is one thing that you worry about, that you feel is out of your control?

6. Write about one or more of the following:

    a. Is there a way that you have a limited amount of control that you don't normally recognize?

    b. If you are going to acknowledge a lack of control and learn to let go, how might you think differently about that situation, event, or individual?

c. What other areas of your professional or personal life are in your locus of control that you might use to help in your thinking about this area?

The Way of the Warrior

Your office cubicle is your familiar present-day work situation. You recognize many of the people around you, but like you, most of them are discontent with their daily work routines. You have spent years, possibly a lifetime at your cubicle but you also know that to stay there any longer would mean your career would stagnate and die.

Although familiar, you have outgrown your job and overall work-related performance, and many aspects of your work no longer resonate with you. You know that a better life exists elsewhere, so you make the decision to leave behind what no longer serves you as you prepare for the most important journey of your lifetime.

As a warrior you know that you will meet with resistance as you travel along your path because others may not understand your mission or respect your desire for change. Others will make attempts to throw the warrior off of their path, but the warrior understands that others are often threatened by their decision to move on. As the warrior, you continue to make plans to depart on your journey to a better career.

Warriors have to make difficult decisions at times, and sometimes the choice must be to leave people and work-related routines behind. The warrior recognizes, however, that those choices are made out of a pure desire to create positive change, both for the self and for others.

You begin to prepare to leave your cubicle and enter the unknown, leaving everything that no longer serves you behind.

A Humble Beginning

You are a warrior, standing just outside of a doorway to a huge skyscraper. You have already traveled long and far, yet you know the journey is really just beginning. You are driven to climb the corporate ladder because you know that the journey to the summit is also a professional desire that you feel drawn to and staying in the same position that you are currently in only creates stagnation and professional discordance.

You have many leadership skills that have not been utilized or recognized by your peers or supervisors. You have outgrown your current position and seek to better not only yourself, but others as well. The journey has not been easy, and yet you know that the hardest part of the journey lies ahead.

You stand next to the green banner. You know that the banner represents movement and to make the journey of the warrior, you move forward in your quest to become the authentic leader within.

As you stand in the near complete darkness outside of the darkened office building, you see the summit or executive suite shining brightly above you in the distance. Although people surround you, they seem lost and directionless in their careers, stumbling to find their own way.

You know that you must make the journey to the summit yourself as it is the only way that will lead to authentic leadership.

This will also be a journey to leader others, and it will be worth the difficult climb.

With a single first step, you move tentatively forward and upward, as you begin to climb the stairwell of the office building.

The warrior's quest is to travel to the top and reach the summit. Along the way, the warrior needs to be aware that she or he will face many obstacles and challenges. The warrior acknowledges this but does not question the path. They simply trust that they are being guided. Warriors begin their journey prepared for the adventures and adversities that life brings. With a single step, they begin to climb, with the understanding that the long, difficult, and rewarding journey leads back to the leader within.

Phase 1:
Commitment to Change

4:00 p.m. – Friday

The end of another work week, yet rather than tying up loose ends at your desk, you find yourself in the stairwell of your office building, burning off extra energy and trying to clear your head. You should be excited! What better way to end the week than to have your boss tell you that you have been promoted.

You are excited, of course. You've waited years for this and the position sounds perfect for you. It has been years since you started working for this employer, and you feel confident about all of your contributions over that time. This is clearly the recognition that you deserve—and recognition that you feel has been a long time coming.

As you climb more stairs, you reflect on how fortunate you are. You have a supportive supervisor, great clients, and rewarding work. In every respect, the past five or so years have gone extremely well for you.

But you're also anxious.

You would love to share the good news with your team. But the reality is that, like in the case of many promotions, you have team members who have been passed over for the opportunity. While they will find out soon enough about the promotion, it does not seem right to share the news with them this afternoon.

There will also be significant new responsibilities that will come along with your promotion. Both you and your boss are more than confident that you are up to the task, but there's also a lot of uncertainty. Combine those new job duties with a new office, and new colleagues and it feels as though you're entering an entirely new world.

On the one hand, you feel well-prepared for the opportunity in the sense that you have watched friends and colleagues getting promoted over the years. You feel as though you have a solid understanding of the risks and rewards that come with promotion. You know what to expect.

As much as anything, though, you also have a great appreciation of how important first promotions can be: you have seen some of your colleagues use them as a way of launching very successful careers. You have seen others struggle to the point that their careers have never fully recovered from poor decisions and mis-steps. It is clear to you that there is a lot riding on this promotion, and so perhaps it should come as no surprise that you're anxious about what next Monday is going to bring you.

§

You begin your new promotion with nothing but a promise and a commitment to yourself that you will do everything within your power to be successful. This will be but the first step on your journey to the summit: a rich and rewarding career. With that resolve, and the fears of the previous week in the past you are eager to begin and face the new challenges before you.

You find that the path is easy and enjoyable at first. Your boss was right to promote you: every decision, every footstep feels right and effortless as you soon forget your old cubicle and the confinement and limitations that you felt in your old position.

Although it may be some years off in the future, the executive suite, the pinnacle of your career, appears closer than ever before. As with many things in life, however, you will soon learn this is only a temporary illusion.

As you settle into your position, the decisions become more complicated and small obstacles seem to grow in size every day. You find yourself retreating frequently to the comfort of climbing the stairs between the floors of the building as a means of escape. There's something about the mindlessness of the steps that help you to clear your head so that you can focus on the difficult decisions you are faced with nearly every day.

After climbing for some time, your mind begins to clear. You notice a light overhead, and it reassures you that you are on the right path with your career, and you feel refreshed and eager to continue on your journey.

§

You realize that you have already grown significantly in your professional life. You have come to realize the importance of starting every day by giving thanks for new beginnings, new opportunities, and the gratitude for what you have. You have learned to recognize the importance of beginning every day with hope, optimism and a fresh perspective—no matter the challenges that may lie in your path.

The stairwell isn't your only solace when you need to clear your mind. When you walk outdoors, the power and strength of your office building is reflected in the long, tall and straight steel lines, the towering glass windows. The building dominates the local skyline, dwarfing all of the others nearby—a comforting symbol of strength and perseverance in your own professional life.

Your career and this journey are well under way, and there is no turning back. Thoughts of failure and returning to the past get actively pushed to the back of your mind, or they would hold you hostage and render you immobile and paralyzed with fear. Climbing forward requires courage and a resolute spirt, and you almost always find your confidence growing once you take that first step in the morning.

With your daily best efforts and intentions, you find that the way forward nevertheless becomes steeper, your leather messenger bag heavier with work at the end of each day, and your steps and progress slow. The air feels as though it is tightening around you.

More often than not, you find yourself alone at work, the building eerily silent except for your own inner voices that tell you to turn back, to take the easier path. The voices aren't entirely your own, they're the voices of past colleagues, supervisors, and others in your life that you fear you will let down if you fail.

As you work, you focus on your own inner voice, which grows in confidence as you learn to listen. You remind yourself to continue this journey, and with resolve to march onward and upward.

When you look up from your work, you realize that hours have passed. Restless, you take to the stairwell before calling it a night and going home. The lights are dim, and the stairwell feels as though it narrows around you as you climb the familiar stairs. You leave tracks on the cement of the dusty stairs with every tired step. The stairs feel abandoned and ill-used, littered with scraps of paper and the remnants of an abandoned repair project.

In spite of the clutter, you focus to clear your mind, resolute in your decision to have accepted this promotion and advance your career. You take time to reflect on the next steps that you will need to take so that you do not get stagnant in this position.

Although it is not common for you to do so, you contemplate the life and the career that you left behind you earlier in the year as you continue hiking up the stairs of the huge office building. But you grow tired and decide to pause briefly to rest.

You find yourself on a floor of the building where you haven't been before and discover nothing but barren rooms. You sit down on the dirty floor. You look at the hallway in front of you and consider the life that you have left behind. A voice tells you that it isn't productive, but you cannot help but consider your previous life and question if you should just return to your cubicle, and to your colleagues.

Stepping out of that nostalgia, you recognize that there is nothing in that old way of life for you anymore. You know that you need to resist those voices that describe a non-existent past and return optimistically to a better life and career that you know pull you forward if you will let it.

After a short amount of time, you stand and dust the dirt off of your pants. Looking down, you notice something on the floor nearby: carved into the base of the concrete floor is a symbol that you do not recognize. It appears to be a series of three interlocking triangles.

You suspect that the symbol should have some significance, but you do not understand what it is. You briefly take note of it, but ultimately dismiss it as graffiti and return to the stairwell.

The brief stop was hardly restful as the stairs feel steeper and darker than you remember them, but you continue up the interior of the building. As you are growing weary, ready to go home for the week, you recognize that your thoughts of failure and returning to your previous life are nothing but self-sabotage to prevent you from moving forward in your career.

Exhausted from the climb, and knowing that it's late in the day, you resolve to reach the next landing. Before you do, you notice a side stairwell continues just above you. You're uncertain which way to go, and you briefly panic as to which steps to take. Your instinct is to dash back down the stairwell to your old familiar place and job. However, the decision feels like it is about more than that: it's about resisting the pull of the familiar in the face of new challenges. It's about having the courage to look more closely at a new situation and assess it carefully and thoughtfully.

    Faced with two directions to take, you recognize that one appears to be more inviting and easier to follow. You have learned, though, that life often presents itself in the form of paradoxes, and that what appears to be the easiest path, may actually turn out to be the most difficult. With this in mind, you know you should not just choose to just take the easier path.

Your head swirls with the uncertainty of the decision, and the desire to leave the stairwell and go home for the weekend. If you choose the wrong path, it could lead you further away from the next landing. Completely alone, you know intuitively that you have to remain still, listen to your inner voice for guidance, before deciding on your next path forward.

Quietly and subtly at first, an inner voice whispers at first, then grows in strength. As a warrior you understand the unseen world of intuition and you honor its guidance as you finally choose your path forward, trusting that it will bring you safely to the next landing, your next destination.

Weary, you continue your climb. The stairwell changes and becomes increasingly alien to you. On a normal day, you seldom have the time to climb this high. You remain mindful of each step and every breath, careful not to fall. You simply focus on the barren walls and steps that surround you.

Just as you struggle to take your next step, you spot the landing just above you. Encouraged, you pick up the pace and follow the staircase, feeling a sense of relief. Now is not the time to stop and rest, so you press forward, exhausted, frustrated and eager to be out of the stairwell and back in the main part of the office with the few co-workers who remain in the building late in the afternoon with you.

You find yourself suddenly angry with yourself because you have climbed this high in the stairwell, and emotions overwhelm you as you stomp around the empty landing, hoping to rest briefly. You are furious but then stop dead in your tracks.

Standing still in the moment, before you focus on the task at hand, you will the anger to leave your body. It's okay, you tell yourself, this is just a part of life. Warriors do not have the expectation that everything will always go the way that they expect or want them to go. Although a difficult and challenging lesson to learn, you recognize there will be times when you will be forced to create a new life, move to a new home, or to take a new job. This is still one of those times as you continue to settle into your new job and responsibilities.

You calm yourself as best you can, take a deep breath and call back your energy as you lean against the wall of the landing and rest briefly.

Although this has to be a temporary stop, you use the opportunity to both rest and reflect on your thanks and gratitude for how far you have come. You also remind yourself that, as with these stairs, you are not the only person to have made this particular journey. There are others who are making their own personal pilgrimages to the top of the building.

Whether they have come before you, or may follow later, your fellow travelers are all attempting to become leaders, and all are making the same climb to the summit. You know that some will succeed, and others will not. You also know that when you see them some look exhausted and worn down from the climb. Others, energized.

Knowing that you can choose to give in to exhaustion or find an inner source of energy for the climb, you feel a brief moment of weakness. However, you do not allow your mind to sabotage your journey: you have made up your mind. You focus on the journey ahead and remind yourself that you are in the difficult process of creating a new life, and the next step in your career, for yourself.

You remember a neglected water bottle in your messenger bag, pull it out and take a short drink. The water is lukewarm but surprisingly refreshing as it also serves to ease your mind. You feel somewhat rested from the walk up the stairs, and the confusion of the multiple paths that you could have selected.

With your mind starting to clear, you finally leave the building for the night. On your way out of the building, you feel a physical jolt overtake your body. You panic as your mind races and you rush to the comfort of your car.

Sitting behind the wheel, you take a deep breath, trying to center yourself again. Everything is silent around you. Afternoon has settled into early evening and the night is already darker than the darkest of nights that you can remember. Your mind suddenly bombards you with thousands of questions that you have yet to fully consider.

Why did you leave your cubicle and the comfort of your previous job?

Will you make a good leader?

Was leaving your old position a mistake?

Will you make it to the summit, or will this promotion be your own undoing?

Will you succeed?

Will you fail?

How will you know?

Questions swirl in your head as you sit in your car, temporarily paralyzed from all of the unanswered questions that you face at this point in your life and career.

These questions, and many like them, are not uncommon when making life changes. We all hear doubts and negative voices from our past that tempt us to abandon new ways of life and return to our old, more familiar ways. However, as warriors, we recognize that this is nothing but self-sabotage. We have to learn to replace those negative, destructive thoughts with positive self-dialogue that shifts our energy away from doubt back to aspirational optimism about our futures.

As you start your car, you remind yourself and recommit to the change in your life that has already been set in motion. Reassuring yourself of your own role in those positive changes in your life, you feel a returning sense of peace and the panic finally starts to subside. You give thanks to your strong inner self that continues to serve as your guide, and remind yourself that you possess the self-confidence and strength of self that you will need for the journey ahead.

You settle into your drive, watching the skyline of the city fade behind you knowing that Monday will bring a new day, full of new challenges. You are comforted in the awareness that you will continue on your warrior's path. The worries and the conflict from the week slowly fade from memory.

A Warrior's Checklist

Gratitude

1. Begin each day with gratitude. Identify one thing in your life, no matter how large or small, that you can truly say you are grateful for.

2. Share your gratitude with at least one other person.

3. Identify one technique or approach that will help ensure that you maintain that one thing in life for which you are grateful.

First Steps

1. Identify the one thing that may be causing you the most anxiety about your day.

2. What one action or decision might you make early in the day that would reduce that anxiety in the future? The source of your anxiety may focus on you individually or may be a step that you take to resolve the issue that concerns you.

3. Take action, and also take time to reflect on your choices. What worked well for you? What didn't work so well? (that

happens sometimes!) What will you adjust and do differently if you need to in the future?

The Power of Others

1. Identify one person in your life who believes in you.

2. What do they see in you that inspires their confidence?

3. What can you do to strengthen your own confidence in those same attributes?

Nostalgia

1. What do you miss from your previous life, before your current position or promotion? Why do you miss it?

2. Are there aspects of that previous life that you can preserve in your new position?

3. Are there aspects of that previous life that you need to learn to let go?

Phase 2:
A Path of Transformation

On a personal and professional level, it's been a particularly challenging year for you. Not only have you been distracted by issues at home that prevent you from doing your best work, but nothing at work seems to be going quite your way either. Although you can't quite put a finger on anything in particular, your boss has asked that you produce a Performance Improvement Plan *to address performance concerns that she has for you. You have always prided yourself on your work and do not take the news well. Shaken, you question whether you even want to put together the* Performance Improvement plan, *or if this might be your supervisor's way of just asking you to leave. It feels like it is going to be a very long week indeed.*

§

Already feeling the stress of a new week, you decide that finding a quiet corner in an empty conference room will help you to collect your thoughts and reflect on the early morning conversation that you just had with your supervisor. The conference room is in a quiet, out of the way corner of your floor, and is seldom used. An interior room, you leave the lights out. The dim light is a welcome respite from an office that is already beginning to buzz with the work of the day.

As you sit in the quiet of the grey light, you suspect that there may not be a right or a wrong path here. You recognize that this is probably just a temporary setback and that each leaders' journey is individual and unique. No two paths to the summit of the skyscraper or executive suite will ever be the same, nor should they. In the experience of writing up a *Performance Improvement Plan*, perhaps there will be an opportunity to learn and grow.

Sometimes alternate pathways that appear to briefly lead away from the end goal are a necessary part of the journey. Such paths can lead the warrior around otherwise seemingly impassible obstacles that aren't always immediately evident. Apparent setbacks are just another paradox that warriors need to understand and contend with.

    Warriors recognize this kind of paradox as having an element of truth. When walking a dangerous, unknown, or unstable path, they sometimes have to reroute themselves to safety on another path to quickly avoid potential pitfalls that may lie ahead of them. Some of those pitfalls can include office politics, the crossing of ethical boundaries, unfair decision making and toxic work conditions. These types of situations never manifest themselves in quite the same way in any given organization or at any given time, so a true leader needs to learn to adapt to whatever situation she finds herself in.

After sitting for some time, you feel the energy levels in the building grow, and you can hear the low humming of the workday as it gets into full swing. You feel the stress of the day, and the work ahead of you, settle into your chest and around your shoulders. Returning to your office, you stop for a quick drink of water and notice something that a co-worker probably dropped without even knowing. Upon closer inspection, you see that it is an old, battered business card. You pick up the card and read it.

The card belonged is that of a previous member of your team who recently left the company.

You fondly remember him as a work friend and a colleague who made a significant impact on both you and the organization. Now, however, he is gone, removed from his position. You are unaware of the details but understand that he was unfairly forced into an early retirement. You absently place the business card into your shirt pocket and head back to your office. You contemplate your previous colleague and your own path when you suddenly realize an opportunity that you had not considered until this morning.

If you hadn't been confronted this morning with the need to write a *Performance Improvement Plan* you might not have considered that you might actually have the opportunity to step into your colleague's previous role within the organization. You recognize that part of the stress that has led you here, has been the result of added work and responsibility over the past couple of months.

Perhaps your conversation with your boss this morning is a blessing in disguise as it has helped you to realize that this might be an opportunity for personal or professional growth, instead of the diversion or even misdirection that you thought it might be originally. Tentatively, you make the decision to forge ahead and accept whatever arrives next for you. You choose to see the positive in your conversation with your boss and look forward, once again, to the possible opportunities that lay before you.

In finding that seemingly inconsequential little business card, you realize that you are largely unconcerned with diverging from your original path or plan because leaders intuitively know that life requires exploration and stretching out into the unknown. New experiences are often found on shifting and changing paths that provide necessary growth and change when and where one least expects it. You recognize that this is one of those opportunities.

You decide to accept the challenge of stepping into a new role again although it will take you away from what you thought was your intended career path. You trust that you are being guided purposefully in a new direction.

You pause outside of your office door briefly as you prepare yourself to enter this new phase of your career, yet you still can't help but to question if it will be right for you.

You experience a moment of fear as old negative thought patterns emerge. You question why you would divert from your original path. Are you making the right choice?

Your energy spirals back and forth, emotions rise and then fall, but you trust that you were guided off your path for a reason. You focus on your past successes, and release your fears as you ready yourself to seek the new position.

As you step metaphorically onto your newly detoured path, you recognize that you will have to shed some of your old ways, and thinking patterns, as you prepare for what you hope will be a new opportunity. The earlier nervousness and fear start to fade, and you feel a sense of inner peace and calm start to take over.

§

The day you learned about writing a *Performance Improvement Plan* and you recognized that it was time to reflect and adjust your plans have faded with the distraction of several years of work. However, you have begun to grow tired of work demands and begin to doubt your decision to diverge from your original path. You recognize that you have gained valuable managerial skills but have come to realize that you have grown considerably in that time.

You have grown weary in the routines of your current position and feel that you have far more to offer your colleagues and organization. Although the position is no longer fulfilling, you recognize that staying in that position does offer security and stability. It makes you feel conflicted, but to stay in a dead-end job will only cause you to lose those personal qualities that you have gained over the past couple of years. When you reflect on your job title of Manager, even if it has only been for a brief period of time, it reminds you of the people and jobs who have been a part of your life's journey that you have left behind over the years.

The warrior knows that a significant life lesson is one of never-ending transformation and change. Every moment offers the opportunity for movement and change, and the chance for learning and expansion in new areas of personal growth or career direction. The choices are not always easy to make, but sometimes hard and painful. Regardless, they always have the potential to lead to personal and professional growth.

Somehow your day has quickly slipped away from you, and fear lodges in your throat as you look around the desolate office environment and you further question this point in your career.

Why are you climbing the career ladder?

Are you climbing for the right reasons?

Where do you think the ladder will really take you?

Could you be happy staying in your current role?

You end a busy day and week, contemplating the decisions that have gotten you to this point in your career and life, but find no easy answers.

As you prepare to leave work, a weeping employee brings you back to the present moment. As you pass through the office space, you see her being escorted from her desk, a solitary cardboard box in hand of personal belongings, by a security guard. She has worked for the organization for almost thirty years. Fear grips your soul. You thought you were alone in the building, but you are not. You panic and race for the exit, not wanting to have to face the employee.

You have nowhere to go other than past her cubicle and the security guard. But then you realize you are not running from the immediate situation as much as from decisions about your own career and self. In your confused and exhausted state at the end of the day, you are unsure if you are merely running away from the security of your current position or running toward something even better and richer with new opportunities?

When warriors are faced with danger or potential pitfalls, they resist reacting emotionally, or from running from fear, and stop to pause to listen carefully and carefully to higher guidance as to what to do. Decisions like these seldom come along, and often appear without warning, and with little or no guidance from others. It is no wonder that they can be intimidating to consider.

As you pause in your flight, you look around and see you have reached the empty stairwell to the parking ramp just a short floors below you, yet the crying continues behind you. Tired, you slump against the wall, knowing that you will have some difficult decisions to make and that only you can make them.

Your hands sink down briefly onto the hard, concrete floor. You question what you just witnessed back in the office. You try to clear your mind knowing that the corporate landscape can be an illusion at times, and fraught with dangers at others. Some people spend their lifetimes trying to climb a summit that they never get to, while others may climb for all of the wrong reasons. You recognize that life can be harsh and no matter how hard you climb or how high, you are not exempt from the struggles of the everyday work warrior.

You start to pull yourself up off the floor when you feel something underneath your hand. As you pull the small object out of a crack in the concrete, you see that it is a little fob that probably fell off from someone's keychain. It shines brightly in the palm of your hand.

You recognize the little metal figure and the three inscribed triangles and know that it is a symbol of power and it brings you comfort.

Knowing that nothing in life is coincidental, the figure has great significance to you.

You acknowledge that the object was placed in your path for a reason, to remind you that warriors have the power to lead, but only if they choose it.

You open up your messenger bag and place the fob inside for safe keeping.

You begin the descent again. Your feet feel heavy on the concrete steps and each step you take becomes harder, but you carry on, ready to end your week.

You sense that the next landing is nearby and just as you struggle to take your next step, you spot a red banner hanging from the wall. You feel paradoxically that you have made it halfway to the summit on your journey to becoming the warrior.

A Warrior's Checklist

Tools for the Journey

Choose an exercise or activity that helps you to center your mind and body when you need a quick break from work. Practice it at least once every day. Your activity could include:

- Mindfulness
- Breathing exercises
- Yoga
- Physical exercise

Self-Reflection

Whether it is a formal activity or otherwise, it is always an opportunity for growth to think about our behaviors and thoughts, and how we might continue to improve ourselves. The challenge, sometimes, is knowing where to even begin with that process of reflection.

1. Think about a colleague, past or present, who you value. Choose one attribute associated with their behavior or way of approaching things.

2. In the behavior of that colleague, what might you emulate?

3. Unfortunately, we don't want to emulate the behavior of all of those around us. Choose a colleague who frustrates you for some reason. Identify one source of that frustration.

4. Given that source of frustration with a colleague, is there any way that your own behavior might reflect or mirror similar behavior? Choose one tangible way that you might modify that behavior.

Taking Stock of Behaviors

1. As you think about your next promotion or opportunity, what one attribute do you think others see in you that makes you most promotable?

2. How can you continue to develop that attribute or skill to ensure that you are a strong candidate?

3. Of those things in your control, what one attribute or skill might be holding you back the most?

4. How might you develop or enhance the weakness you identified in the previous step and turn it into a strength that will help lead to promotion or new opportunities?

Phase 3: Navigating Treacherous Water

You really love the job that you do for your organization! The only challenge that you have is that your boss is extremely toxic. You don't have any specific, personal concerns or issues, but she is constantly attacking the members of your team, accusing them of under-performing and making mistakes they are not responsible for making. You're not sure if she's covering for her own weaknesses or not, but you're certainly worried that you could easily end up being the next target of her ire.

§

You pull your car into a parking place at work, and take a deep breath, exhaling last week's stale energy. The past is behind you. You are grateful for a new day and a new beginning. More importantly, you promise yourself that you won't let issues with your boss get to you this morning. Your team has some significant deadlines looming in front of them later in the week, and you need everyone, including yourself, focused on meeting those dates and not disappointing a key client.

You stand and stretch beside your car in the silence of the parking ramp, noting the start of the business day. Both you and your team all enjoy starting the day early, before most of the rest of your co-workers arrive at work. You remind yourself that it is early morning moments like these, that you enjoy the most because they allow you to stop and reflect, gather yourself, and plan for the day ahead and the challenges that it will bring.

You have always welcomed new possibilities and new challenges that you have faced in the business world. It has always been your own level of resolve that separates you from those around you. Whenever your team, or a supervisor, has looked to someone to take on a challenge, you have always been the first one there, volunteering to do what no one else is willing to take on.

It is with exactly that kind of attitude that you reflect upon the red banner that you saw hanging in the stairwell when you left work at the end of last week. Although the banner was hung there to add a little bit of color and life to an otherwise drab wall, you also remind yourself that red represents power and strength. But as with anything in life, the banner and the color red have another side. Red, you recognize, also represents danger. In spite of your unwavering confidence in your team this week, you know that your boss has become increasingly challenging to deal with, blaming your team for mistakes that they haven't made, and accusing them of not performing up to her expectations. You love your team and the stability of your current position, but the work environment your boss has created has become toxic to the point where you question if you can still manage to continue work there any longer. For the time being, and for the sake of your team, you focus on the positive side of the red banner, choosing strength for the challenges you will face this week.

You pause for just a short time longer, take a deep breath, and prepare yourself for what is sure to be an extremely difficult week, full of stress, difficult work, and long hours. As a professional warrior who has been through times like this in the past, you know that taking care of your body is essential to your personal and professional success. You will need to remind yourself on a regular basis this week to take time out to focus on your physical well-being, so you don't burn out.

Without a healthy body, you know that your mind will be negatively affected. As you continue your climb to the professional summit, you will need to remain strong in body, mind, and spirit to achieve your goals. As you and your team seem to be experiencing all too regularly, an unhealthy leader leads unintentionally through their negative example. Not just for your own sake, but for the sake of your team, you know that you need to take good care of yourself this week.

As often as you are able, you will remind yourself and make sure that you listen carefully to what your body needs. Warriors listen closely to their physical needs as much as their intellectual and emotional ones. They know that nutrition, exercise, and rest are essential elements to staying healthy.

The warrior does not disrespect his or her body with alcohol or drugs, nor do they consume unhealthy foods. They do not give in to temptations that sabotage their physical well-being. Instead they make choices that empower their bodies, create strength, and promote endurance. You also understand that stress this week will lead you to be tempted to give in to unhealthy choices. However, you know full-well that you will need to work hard to resist those temptations and remain strong.

As you prepare to leave the parking garage, you meditate on gratitude for the new day, for a strong team, and success in the challenges that lie ahead of you. You acknowledge that the journey will be difficult. With that knowledge in mind you step firmly and resolutely back onto your path and begin the climb refreshed.

§

By the middle of the week, you have thoughts of giving up. Even the strongest and most resolute warrior sometimes experiences moments of weakness. So far, you and your team have faced nothing but challenges, setbacks and busy work. Your deadlines are looming ever larger on the horizon, and you have lost hope that you will meet those deadlines.

You take a moment's pause at your desk and remind yourself of how you started the work week, in quiet contemplation at the side of your car, reassuring yourself of the importance of taking care of yourself this week. You readily admit that you haven't made the best choices so far this week. In your messenger bag, you recall having healthy and nutritious snacks and bottled water from home, to be consumed throughout the day, and to help you avoid other less healthy temptations. Warriors know that nutrients and hydration are essential. Without a strong physical body, you won't make it to the summit, let alone meet your deadlines at the end of the week.

Unhealthy bodies also lead to unhealthy minds, and often even lead to negative decision making. More than most weeks, you feel especially challenged to remain mentally focused and prepared to help your team. It doesn't help that you have no support from your own supervisor, and you have done your best to try and shield your team from those stresses and office politics.

You make a conscious effort to step away from your desk every hour or so and to exercise each day, knowing that your body needs movement to stay healthy. Even when it feels like you don't have time to exercise, you remind yourself of the value of a healthy body.

A continued focus on health and well-being brings new-found energy into every cell of your body. After a solid workout, you have never regretted the short time away from your office, and you almost always return refreshed and ready to take on the challenges that face you.

Back at your desk, you settle however briefly into solitude. You remain uncertain about the future or your path ahead, but you no longer cling to the past. You simply enjoy the present moment. The warrior knows that mental energy spent in the past, or on those things outside of one's control, is wasted and only keeps them tied to a life that no longer exists.

Instead, warriors stay focused on thoughts of the present, as well as future goals. They remain focused on their abilities to lead others through adversity. They trust in their own skills and know that they have the ability to positively lead others.

As your deadline relentlessly approaches, you realize that the challenge ahead feels steeper and more treacherous with every passing hour. In spite of the risk to you and your team, or perhaps because of them, you pause briefly to think, staring off into space, trying to collect your thoughts and plan your next steps. You recognize the danger in looking back and make the decision that you can't settle for failure. Failure will not serve either you or your team.

You stop abruptly.

You sit in silence, becoming one with your surroundings. You close your eyes and feel the power and pull of the others around you, and the work that you are trying to complete. Although you feel as though you are symbolically climbing a mountain, wisdom tells you that mountains can be shattered with lightning, eroded by time, or bored through straight to their inner cores. But those very same mountains remain resolute, strong and intact. The image of the mountain reminds you that you are also strong in your own way, so you choose to keep moving toward your destination knowing that you have the power and strength to get through this journey. Today, this day, is all that you need to focus on, and you will remind your team that the same holds true for them.

Wisdom and your past experience also tell you that the path to becoming a great leader can be unpredictable at times. People can be removed from office, they can fall into workaholism, and they can become unpopular with their colleagues and be forced to step down. That, however, is not your course. You know that the path to becoming an executive can be a lifelong career climb that can sometimes result in the painful realization that the journey was not what the warrior thought it would be. Along the way, the warrior might become disappointed and full of regrets. Life often appears unpredictable and full of unknowns. True warriors, though, know that the larger regrets in life come from not making the journey, but instead in not taking appropriate risks.

You work silently for a few hours, trying to help your team navigate the final stretches of your project so you can meet your deadline. But a storm approaches, and you don't think it is avoidable. Once again, it feels like your team is being sabotaged. While you had hoped this storm would pass, you recognize the need to act quickly and with resolve.

Over the years, you have learned that you think best with a change of scenery and a breath of fresh air. You decide to leave your desk and take a short walk. Because the stairwell is almost always deserted, and a good place to walk and think, you begin climbing stairs. After a couple of flights of stairs, you realize that your nervous energy had gotten the better of you!

You sit down on a step and rest, when without warning, raindrops begin to leak into the stairwell. At first you are not that startled as the rain settles beneath your feet, but then the rain outside becomes heavier and even more droplets begin to pelt the floor.

You become alarmed as water begins to trickle down the stairs. You stand alone in the narrow hallway looking up at the ceiling. You don't know what to do. Should you go back down and warn someone about the leaking roof, or should you go forward and upward? What you might choose is unclear, but you believe that your intuition is guiding you for a reason, so you run further up the stairs, as it feels like the walls are closing in around you.

A bolt of lightning strikes overhead and lights up the skylight above you. Water falls in rivulets from the ceiling as the skylight cracks and collapses from the pounding wind and hail. Your mind races and worry about the storm begins to mix with your fears about work.

Would it just be easier to leave your job and the stress of a toxic work environment behind?

Should you instead follow your intuition and try and solve the underlying issues with your boss?

What are you truly seeking through all of this stress and effort?

Will you ever succeed and make it to the summit?

Are you meant to lead, or are you part of the problem?

You start to dash up the stairs even faster, although you have no idea what lies ahead. You trip on the step and fall face first into the grimy water on the next landing. You pick yourself up, wipe your hands briefly on your rumpled suit, and resume sprinting up the stairs. You have no idea if you are running toward security or away from it, so you come to an abrupt stop.

The water rains down on you and you think it can't get much worse than this.

You are alone in the stairwell, but even more alone than you have ever been in your life as a professional. You see no way out. You're unsure if you should stay and confront your boss or accept the inevitable and leave the organization. Either way, you recognize that you cannot just continue with the status quo. Something has to change, and you need to find the courage to enact that change.

You contemplate your life and career choices and start to question why this is happening to you. But as you have done when faced with similar challenges in the past, you call forth your inner warrior. You recognize that negative thoughts carry destructive energy and you shift your thoughts, much like the storm that rages outside your office. You have both the wisdom and the ability to shift yourself out of the current situation toward a resolution. A good leader actively manages during chaotic and destructive times, understanding what remains in their control.

After a short time, you choose to move on, as the stairwell still feels to be closing in on you, even if the thought is not entirely rational. You can see the stormy dark sky through the skylights in the stairwell but you continue up the stairs unhindered.

The stairs lead you quickly around a series of corners until a landing opens up before you and you see relief ahead: a door to another floor of the building. However the door seems seldom used, and refuses to open all the way for you. The rain from the storm has leaked around some of the other skylights and has made the stairwell slippery with water and dirt, and you don't feel that it is safe returning the way that you came.

A rusted pole leans against the corner, opposite the door. Your sense is that you might use it to pry open the door, and escape to a higher floor.

A slight panic sets in, as you see storm clouds passing quickly through the overhead skylight above. Wisdom tells you to stop fighting against the door. Just as you release control on the pole, something in the doorframe shifts, falls to the floor, and the door opens before you. You set aside the pole and walk through onto the office floor. No one seems to notice you, let alone that you are soaking wet from your encounters in the stairwell.

    The warrior knows that in life, resistance always leads to suffering and when engaged in a power struggle, energy is lost and depleted in the sheer act of resisting. As with the door, the warrior's lesson is to let go and move with the flow of life. The end result is often change that is larger and better than we may have ever anticipated. Although difficult, attempting to hold onto what no longer is or what no longer serves us, only results in pain and frustration. Warriors know when to let go.

Cold and wet, you try to wipe yourself off and begin to search for a place to rest and dry off.

You return to your office and sit in your chair. Your thoughts return to your team and the looming deadline you are still trying to meet, even though the odds appear stacked against you. You remind yourself of the paradox of letting go of the pressure on the pole in the stairwell. Perhaps if you also learn to let go of control of your project, your team will have the freedom to move forward and complete it successfully and on time. While this lesson is yours and yours alone, you are also mindful that your journey has a strong influence on others and will impact their own successes and failures.

Just as you prepare to return to the work at hand, the storm passes as quickly as it started, and you fall back into a comforting rhythm of work. The day draws to a close. Although you don't know precisely what tomorrow will bring or where you will end up, you do take comfort in knowing that this is the way of the warrior: learning to let go is as essential sometimes as asserting control. The path to leadership is full of challenges and you have overcome a crucial one today.

A Warrior's Checklist

Treacherous Situations

Recognizing, dealing with and avoiding treacherous situations can take several forms including:

- Recognizing the signs of danger before it happens
- Identifying where you are losing energy
- Noting addictions, which may interfere with your personal and or professional life
- Taking care of your physical body

- Identifying triggers in your own behavior
- Self-sabotaging behaviors

Evaluating a Situation

1. Identify a situation that is causing you difficulty. List one way that you resist dealing with that situation.

2. What is one action that you can take today that will help ease that resistance?

3. Describe one approach or emotion that you associate with the situation that you think you would benefit from

when you choose to let it go. If you find it difficult to let go, what can you replace that approach or emotion with that would help you to move forward?

Evaluating Your Role

4. In the situation that you identified above, what is your role?

5. How can you modify your role to be more supportive?

6. Identify one behavior that you believe you should change. How should you change it? How would your team suggest you change?

Evaluating the Roles of Others

7. While we often look inward as warriors and leaders, we recognize that sometimes those around us might also need to change. Think of one individual who might need to change their behavior, attitude, or approach to a problem or project that you share.
8. How would you describe the situation you identified above in a way that would be constructive and non-threatening?

9. How would you affirm at least one approach or action of that team member?

10. If you could only change one action or approach of that team member, what would it be? How will you constructively and actively communicate that change?

Phase 4: Professional Darkness

Over the past twelve months or so, you have been struggling at work. You and your supervisor still aren't communicating well at all, your projects are languishing and—quite frankly—you are not feeling very valued by your organization. You have been looking for an opportunity elsewhere on and off for quite some time and have become frustrated by the lack of interest from prospective employers.

It comes as a big surprise when one of your company's main competitors offers you a position with them. To say that you are eager to leave your current company and position is an understatement at best, and you are more than ready to try something new. On top of it all, this opportunity comes with a significant promotion and a raise. There's just one small problem: although you can't quite pinpoint a specific concern, something just does not feel right about this opportunity. So you question whether you try and remain patient in your current position, hoping that you find something better—or that your fortune turns around in your current position.

Instead, do you risk it all, and remove yourself from what might best be described as a losing situation? Among your many concerns and frustrations, you aren't exactly getting any younger. If there's a time to make a change, you feel as though it's quickly fading away.

§

You awake in the morning, unrested, to the sound of rain outside of your bedroom window. The gentle sound reminds you of your adventure in the stairwell from the day before. You reflect on life's changes and know that at any moment, life can and will change abruptly both personally and professionally. And you are still feeling unsettled about the impending decision to make a career move.

It was a long and sleepless night: normally, you would have expected to not sleep well because of the typical stresses from work, the looming deadlines, the office politics. However, in addition to all of those things, your drive home was anything if not uneventful.

You haven't spoken much about it to anyone, not even to family or friends, but you have been frustrated recently by the fact that you've been considering some kind of career change—but haven't found anything that has worked out.

It was a phone call on the drive home last night changed that: a position that you had been seeking, and that you thought had already been filled, has come through! Although still just a verbal offer of employment, the new position would mean a significant promotion and a raise. You very much enjoyed meeting everyone at the new company when you interviewed a few weeks ago, and you think the work would be both challenging and rewarding.

But in spite of that, something doesn't feel right to you. Call it instinct or a gut feeling, but you tossed and turned most of the night anxiously trying to figure out what seemed out of place with the opportunity. Ultimately you convinced yourself that perhaps it was just the fear of something new and unknown, that was making you uneasy. If nothing else, that thought allowed you to finally fall into a brief, fitful sleep for a couple of hours. With the morning rain and storms, though, the same vague concerns start gnawing at you once again.

On your way out the door later that morning, you collect your messenger bag, anxious to try and make a decision and either remain where you are or begin the next phase of your journey. So far, this is probably the most significant career decision that you have ever needed to make, and you really are not sure how best to proceed, or who to talk to. In spite of the impending decision you also need to get to work. You and your team still have pressing deadlines to meet this week.

When you arrive at the office, you find that you just are not prepared to meet with your team and would like to find a quiet corner to try and clear your mind—if that is even possible this morning. You recall from the day before that there were empty offices a few floors up from where you and your team work—perfect as a location to sit and contemplate your next move without interruption. You have your cell phone, so you aren't concerned that your team won't be able to reach you if it is absolutely necessary.

When you step into the stairwell, you find that it has been thoroughly cleaned and the skylight repaired—everything is intact and as it should be. There is no evidence of the previous day's storms.

As you recalled, when you step out from the stairwell, you spot an abandoned and dark office a few short steps away. It is near the back of the floor, nestled into the shadows. It appears to have been long neglected, but more importantly for you, it is unoccupied and should offer you a quiet place to sit and think for a few minutes.

When you reach the empty office's doorway, you pause briefly. From a practical perspective, you know that your team needs you and you should probably be downstairs at your desk.

But you realize that this empty office is more than just that: this office represents the dark and unknown side of the new job opportunity and the decision that you need to make.

Do you enter?

Do you walk past it, turn and go back to your team and current position?

If you do enter, will you ultimately regret the decision?

You step tentatively into the dark, empty space and stare out the large windows of the office at the city skyline just at the edge of the horizon. For you, this darkened office truly represents the job opportunity that you hope will reward you financially, intellectually, and allow you to escape your current situation. However, the emptiness of the office also causes you to realize what you have been concerned with this entire time: you are certain that it will not fully utilize your leadership skills. While you are certain the new opportunity is a secure job, you are becoming increasingly clear that it will not feed your soul, instill you with a sense of purpose and professional drive, or provide you with the opportunities to lead or to rise up within that organization.

In the darkness of this foreign and little-used office, you recognize that you would most likely be accepting a job offer for all of the wrong reasons. You realize that running from your current situation will only cause you larger problems further on in your career. As much as you had felt compelled to accept this position, your heart and your mind have known all along that you shouldn't accept it, and instead continue your search.

With resolve building around a final decision, you reflect for a brief moment longer in the darkness of the office and take note of the deafening silence of this particular floor of the building. The only thing you hear at the moment is the beating of your own heart. Before your resolve fades, you make a quick phone call and politely decline the offer.

While you have just made a temporary commitment to stay in your current position, a sense of fear grips you again as you finally start to be honest with yourself and face the reality that you have spent years, possibly a decade or more in the wrong position, perhaps even the wrong organization. It is the reality that you may be in the wrong place in your professional life that you realize has been at the root of your uneasiness about the new position. You recognize, ultimately, that you cannot allow previous bad decisions to result in another one. And certainly not at this critical juncture in your career: you need to make sure that you make your next move carefully or it could be disastrous for you, both professionally and personally.

Panic resulting from the enormity of the decision that you have just made, and past mistakes, makes you want to run fleeing from the office building, away from your team and from the deadlines that you face. You force yourself to pause momentarily to assess your current situation and the sense that you feel trapped.

Do you continue in your current position because it is "safe" and has excellent benefits?

Do you try and go back to a previous position that once brought you much more job satisfaction?

Or do you continue your climb to the summit, the executive suite, even if it means leaving the comfort and safety of your current position?

You realize that confidence in making difficult decisions can be fleeting at best and know that you are second-guessing yourself.

Being a warrior, you harness your thoughts and emotions, and collect yourself in an effort to get a hold on your fear, summon back your energy, and ultimately regain a sense of resolve. You decide there has only ever been one option: to move forward.

You remind yourself again that turning down the new position was the right thing to do. You realize that to have taken it would certainly have ended with the early death of your soul, your creativity, and your ability to lead others. You feel as though you have released your fears and are now free to continue your climb toward something better, a leadership role that feeds you with positive energy and resonates deeply from within your true self.

You return to your team and what you find is an uncharacteristically quiet floor. Looking for your team, you accidentally stumble into a meeting that your boss is leading. She looks surprised to see you and stands from where she sits at the head of the table before you can apologize for the interruption.

She stutters a little bit as she says good morning, and you can sense that something isn't quite right in the conference room. Everyone at the table looks ill at ease. Your boss asks if she can speak with you alone.

Once you are together in your office, she quietly shuts the door behind her—something she has never done before.

There is harsh and cruel irony in your decision to have turned down the new job: you and your teammates have all lost your jobs in a large company reorganization. The rest of your team found out their fates while you were standing quietly, alone, and in an empty office just a few dark floors above them. You ask your boss briefly about the fate of the project you were working so hard to complete, only to be told that it, too, was no longer a priority after the reorganization of the company. There doesn't seem to be anything left to say.

As you walk dazedly to your car, your few belongings tucked into your messenger bag, you choke back something that is somewhere between laughter and grief. The harsh irony is that this last decision that you had struggled over for the past couple of days to make has ultimately been made for you. It is unquestionably time to move on to other professional opportunities. The choices you thought you were making earlier in the morning, had in fact already been made for you.

The damp, semi-grey air of the parking ramp feels like a heavy woolen cloak that covers and threatens to suffocate your body and mind. You are in what feels like the darkest night of your soul. You do not see an obvious way ahead, nor do you see the way back very clearly anymore. You are trapped in a void. You resist the urge to panic; you also somehow maintain your inner power and sense of self by willing your mind to remain still.

Wisdom tells you that if you flee, mentally or physically, you could lose yourself and never make it out of what has turned into a disastrous day.

Nothing in your career to this point ever prepared you for this. While you have seen and known others who have lost their jobs, you never in your wildest dreams expected that it would happen to you. And yet, here you find yourself: thinking you had made a careful and calculated decision about your career only to have the rug pulled out from underneath you. You feel betrayed for all of your work and years of commitment to your company.

In allowing your eyes to adjust to the dim light of the parking ramp, you try to adjust your inner self to a new and uncomfortable darkness that threatens to engulf you.

Intellectually, the warrior in you knows not to make decisions out of haste or fear, yet every thread of your being wants nothing more than to flee from the situation.

In the shadows of the parking ramp, you reach quickly and blindly for your car keys, and your fingers brush against the object that you found the week prior in the stairwell. You remove it from your pocket to take a closer look. Although it is old and a bit tarnished from its time in the stairwell, in the dim light you can vaguely make out one word etched faintly into the obscure little object below the interlocking triangles: *vision*.

You suspect the object was a small token given to employees as a symbolic gift for their years of service to the company, or perhaps in recognition for a job well done on an important project. Ironic that you would find it in your pocket this morning. But you also recognize that nothing in life is pure coincidence and that you are being guided down a new path.

Somehow this talisman was meant to be found this morning, so you put it back into your jacket pocket for safe-keeping, preparing to leave work for the very last time.

The short ceiling of the parking ramp feels claustrophobic, but you stay strong as you know that sometimes you have to go through difficult situations to advance and climb the corporate ladder. You remind yourself that career success seldom happens without challenges along the way. You know that those who hang fearfully onto security, benefits or job titles for the wrong reasons will be challenged in many unexpected ways. You try and tell yourself that the layoff was for the best and is a "letting go" that has been a long time coming.

Offices can be lonely, soul sucking places. They can make you physically ill, perpetually exhausted and sap you of all of your energy.

You know that, for all of those reasons, this is not the time to give up, and as a warrior you recognize when it's time to move on in your career and in life. You know that you need to honor your inner warrior, and not give into the fear of what should not been seen as a setback, but merely a transition.

In spite of everything you understand on an intellectual level, you break down any way. You can't see the way forward and the loss of control is devastating. You trusted your inner vision and your decisions earlier in the morning, but now have doubts you will find your way to getting your career back on track. Fear rises like a raging demon, threatening to engulf your very soul.

You have been forced to leave the past behind you but can't see the future that should be in front of you. You are terrified. Even as a warrior, you have suddenly and irrevocably lost your way-in spite of all your best efforts to the contrary. You panic and scream, but no one hears because you are alone. Silence reverberates around you like an abyss. You are inconsolable as you sob in your car, feeling that life has abandoned you. You question your path, your existence, your purpose.

Why did you accept this position in the first place, so many years ago?

Why did you stay so long?

How will you tell your family and friends?

What will it be like to move on losing your benefits and security behind?

How will you pay your bills and provide for your family?

Will you ever regain your inspiration and confidence to make a difference?

Will you get to the top of the summit, the executive suite or will you end your career in a dead-end job?

For that matter, will you even find another job?

The risks before you are significant and feel entirely unknown and insurmountable to you.

Emotionally exhausted, you feel for the object inside your jacket pocket. Grasping it in your hand, you again question what it means. You briefly nod off in front of your steering wheel with the medallion held firmly in your hand.

You dream briefly and fitfully that you are walking even further up the stairwell in your office building, which now stands dark and completely abandoned against the skyline of the city. But in your dream, you somehow have no fear as you almost magically see clearly in the darkness. You move with confidence and trust as you are able to navigate the narrowing hallways that wind further higher toward the building's summit.

Your journey, although conducted in complete darkness, feels easy and effortless as you now see the way ahead. The stairwell becomes surreal and smaller and narrower, but just when you think that the hall is too tight to continue climbing, you see a light shining in the distance above you. You squeeze your way to the top where there is light. Somehow you also know there is a beautiful office that awaits you.

You wake up, knowing that the object in your hand provided you with insight and vision to see through the dark illusion of life.

Although tentatively, you feel ready to continue your journey. You trust that the way forward lies ahead, even if the path isn't perfectly clear to you at the moment.

As you drive, you reflect on the morning's events. You know that the object in the stairwell was put there for the warrior as a reminder that guidance comes in many forms and shapes. The small token allowed you to see in the darkness at a time when you felt like giving up, reminding you that there is always a way out, even when you are truly lost in the darkness of self-doubt and despair. You will not be stuck in this transition and feel confident that you will find something better. It will take some time, but if you can see your own strengths and abilities, other will be able to as well. You acknowledge, too, that if you had stayed in the wrong position, or accepted the wrong offer, you, and your talents, your leadership skills would have continued to go unnoticed and unused.

You anticipate that this may be a time when you may need to accept a job position or opportunity that you do not necessarily want. However, if you do, you remind yourself to take solace in the fact that this is part of the climb that will serve as a catalyst for newfound skills and experiences that ultimately will lead you to the executive suite. Your personal and professional journey is going to be different than accepting or staying in a position that would only lead to self-defeat, despair and a loss of your creative talents.

As you try and will the pain and fear to recede, you know that you have newfound tools to help you through the difficult moments in your career. You feel a renewed sense of self-confidence that you will successfully navigate this transition.

With a sense of hope, you finally drive confidently away from your old office. The rains have stopped, and you can reflect back on the fact that you closed the door to your office for the last time, never to return.

You look once more into the rearview mirror at the office building. Although this is a difficult time in your life, you anticipate that one day you will use your own painful experiences to help others who will face similar challenges in their own careers, and that sounds like reward enough.

The fading shadow of the office behind you serves as a reminder of how life's paths will continue to shift and that the warrior will be pulled down into darkness again someday. However, you know that if you maintain your trust and faith in yourself, even in the darkest of times, you will always find your way out.

You have lived through the dark night of the soul and survived.

A Warrior's Checklist

Vision and Insight

Vison and insight come from many sources. Explore how the following might help you discover more about your inner self:

- Meditation
- Mindfulness
- Time reflecting in nature
- Study of spirituality

Reflection

1. When we are faced with difficult situations, it is

sometimes helpful to reflect on our current role on a project or within an organization. Think back on a difficult work situation that was out of your control.

2. In that situation, describe one aspect that was outside of your control. How did it make you feel? Describe one way that you could have managed your feelings differently than you did at the time.

3. In the same situation, describe a different aspect that was outside of your control, but didn't need to be.

How could you have gained control? How do you think that might have ultimately changed the outcome of that situation?

Spirituality

Reflect upon your spirituality and the role that it plays in your daily life:

- How do you honor your commitment to yourself? How do you do this on a daily basis?
- Have you accepted the call to a spiritual life? If not, what barriers exist? How can you remove them?

- What value in your spiritual path are you willing to share with others?

Phase 5: Climbing Higher

Security is a fickle and fleeting thing. One of the most significant reasons that you had always stayed with your job was safety in knowing that you would always have a job with great benefits. Over the years, as you watched the economy grow and contract, you witnessed friends and colleagues getting laid off and losing their jobs. But you were always secure in your own position. It may not have been the best paying or the most glamorous, but it was safe.

When you suddenly and unexpectedly found yourself out of work, you were confident you would find something quickly. But fortunes changed unexpectedly, and the economy fell suddenly into a recession at almost the same time that you lost your own job.

Your job search has languished. It's not just that you aren't getting call-backs, no one seems to be hiring at all. Financially, you have managed reasonably well so far, but unemployment benefits will be running out soon and your savings are gone. On top of it all, you've extended your credit cards to further help manage your household bills. In another week or two, you fear the situation could turn catastrophic when you are unable to pay your mortgage and the rest of your bills. When that happens, you're not sure what you will do.

§

You start your mornings early and predictably with a handful of friends who meet at the area lake for a short run, and then a cup of coffee and a quick visit. When everyone else leaves for work, you return home where you rely on more rituals to help you make it through the long day. After starting out by searching through the major online job boards, you target a short list of employers to see if there are any openings. As you suspected: nothing.

After an early lunch, you typically transition to what always feels like the more stressful and humiliating part of your search: at least one phone call to a colleague to do a little networking.

Even that doesn't seem to work.

By the end of the day, you wrap up with simple tasks to try and keep your mind off of the impending feeling that you are failing and failing miserably. You make a few difficult decisions about which bills to pay, which of the others will have to be late, update your status for unemployment, and finally finish with a few other small tasks that have gone neglected most of the week. While there is always time and more to do, you find yourself emotionally exhausted and unable to work any longer.

Your old, leather messenger bag sits in the corner of your home office, unopened and neglected since the afternoon that you lost your job. Of course, you should probably put it away. Just seeing the weathered bag contributes to the stress and tension that you feel spreading across your shoulders and throughout your aching body.

It is at least an hour before your spouse gets home from work, and you have some time to kill, but no energy remaining for work. You wouldn't normally go out with friends, but a colleague from your former employer invited you out for a beer with him and a few other of your old co-workers. It's just one beer, and it would feel good to get out of the house and avoid the stress of your job search. You can't afford to go, but you justify it to yourself. It's just once, after all.

Later that night, before you sleep, you tell yourself not to worry that the one beer turned into three or four. You think. It was, after all, just once, and you tell yourself that it won't happen again. You have been under an immense amount of stress, and things can only get better. Everything is fine.

As you start to try and drift off to sleep, you mentally begin to prepare yourself for tomorrow's search. You have learned that the path of a warrior is never straight forward or easy, but an ongoing and continuous ebb and flow of change, much like your climb to the executive suite. Direct routes are always difficult to find, and although few find them, you know that your journey has turned into a lengthier process of experience and hard work. It might take you longer to achieve your goals, but you persuade yourself that everything you seek is ultimately within your reach.

    The next morning, you don't get out of bed to join your friends for their morning run and coffee. It's just one time, you're tired, and in fairness, everyone deserves a day off every now and then. It makes it that much easier to stay in bed because of the nagging headache from the beer the night before.

When you finally do get out of bed to begin your day, you immediately feel a sense of guilt at getting such a late start. Perhaps you'll just accommodate by skipping your afternoon phone calls. It's not like you ever accomplish anything by making those calls anyway.

You take a sip of steaming hot coffee as you sit down at your laptop, and idly start flipping through the same job sites as the day before, and the day before that. Your search seems futile.

You do your best to remind yourself that the warrior will be tested often over the course of her or his journey. This is nothing more or less than a temporary setback that you will overcome.

You know that you have traveled far, but the tests of your resolve apparently are not over yet. The universe will test the warrior in ways that may force her or him to fall off their path and plummet far below. You laugh nervously to yourself, confident that you could not have fallen any further if you had tried. The same worries from the day before slowly start to creep back, and you do your best to keep them at a safe distance so that you can continue to focus on your search.

Warriors expect that tests always lie ahead. You know in your heart and mind that you need to continue to climb, maintaining a mindful eye on the path below you as well as on the one ahead, even when the ultimate destination may not be evidently clear. To be perfectly honest, though, you struggle to see a way forward at all.

You wrap up your day, having prepared yourself the best that you can for the next day. You sleep well through the night and wake up feeling more refreshed. You look forward to the day's journey, reminding yourself that the mistakes of the past couple of days were nothing but minor setbacks in the larger journey that still lay in front of you.

The next morning, you pick up your gym bag which holds a fresh change of clothing and a towel and head out for your morning run and coffee. You barely give your messenger bag a second glance, abandoned and unused for the moment in the corner of your home office.

It's a beautiful early morning, and it mirrors your mood: there isn't a cloud in sight and you feel ready to take on the world.

Your run starts remarkably well in the crisp early morning air, and your steps feel light and easy. But as your turn at the halfway point of the path around the lake, you find that your steps start to get harder, and your breathing becomes measured and heavy. Your friend chooses that exact moment to ask you how your job search is going.

Certainly, you're just feeling a little sensitive, but the tone of the conversation feels overly judgmental—and you start to feel as though you just aren't doing enough with your job search. It's unlike you to ever need to stop and rest when you are out running, but the morning's run just doesn't feel right any longer. You tell your friend to go on ahead without you, and you end up pausing multiple times to catch your breath before your run finally ends, alone.

You take a few minutes to change clothing and clear your mind. Over coffee with your friends, the conversation feels shallow and distant to you, but at least it's safe. No one asks any further awkward questions about your job search. As everyone prepares to leave for work, a colleague offers you a worn copy of a book, *Life Warrior: The Everyday Summit*. You recognize it as a title that was recommended to you some time ago, but you just never quite got around to reading it. Although you don't realize it at the moment, the book will become your guide and companion for the rest of your journey. Like you, the book has its own story along with a variety of tools to help you make the long ascent to your ultimate professional goals. For the time being, though, you thank your friend, and casually drop the book into your gym bag.

On the drive home, your friends are on your mind. The warrior knows that everything and everyone has a story, each uniquely individual. Stories of success are as diverse and unique as each person has their own journey, regardless of where they end up in life. Some journeys are successful, and others less so. When you reflect on your friends and their careers, you take some comfort in knowing that many of them have survived considerable adversity. You know that if they can move forward and thrive, so too can you. More importantly, however, the warrior knows that all journeys carry a variety of lessons with them, and many of those stories will have meaning for you personally if you have the courage and patience to seek them out.

Having returned home later in the morning, you sit in your home office, tired and a bit distracted. Staring out the window, the sky has clouded over, much like your mood. You watch the ever-changing clouds outside and reflect on the many jobs that you have held over the years.

Your mind drifts momentarily away from thinking about your career, and you instead start to daydream about the shapes that appear in the clouds outside of your window. You try to interpret the cloud's shapes and the messages that they might hold. You contemplate their meaning.

Not far from your mind, too, is the conversation with your colleague on your morning run. There are various ways to communicate and you recognize that words can often be used to inspire or to harm others, regardless of whether or not the words are intentional. You also realize that how you hear or receive those words also has power and that how you heard your friend may have been more important than his intentions in asking about your job search. Your reaction to his questions probably said more in mirroring how you felt than anything else.

Positive leaders know to choose their own words wisely and decide how they hear the words of others just as wisely. They want their team, and each individual employee to feel valued and respected. They want them to feel that they are a valued part of the organization, the team or the project so they learn effective ways of communication that leaves the entire team uplifted, feeling heard, understood and ultimately valued.

The most effective leaders are careful not to talk excessively or carelessly, to listen thoughtfully, and not to interrupt others when they are talking because they understand the power of listening, in learning from those with whom they surround themselves. Leaders know that everyone they encounter on their journey has the potential to offer wisdom and guidance. They listen to their co-workers, colleagues, friends, and family carefully.

Warriors also understand the importance of being quiet and introspective each day, even when that means an activity as simple as meditating on the clouds passing by overhead. They go into silent contemplation and allow their minds to become still, clearing all negative thoughts and words from their minds because they know that in silence, clarity often emerges.

By contrast, excessive or racing thoughts have the potential to become toxic to others around you as well as to ourselves. The can keep people stuck in negative patterns of behavior that lead to fear, self-doubt, and uncertainty. They can be devastating and paralyzing.

As you watch the shifting clouds overhead, you drift away even further from your work, and begin to grow tired and even further distracted.

At this point, you no longer reflect on your past jobs, and what has been left behind, but focus on each step, every breath, and the path that lay ahead of you as a means of bring yourself back to the present moment.

Another cloud appears and it grabs your attention. You try to make out its shape and symbolism as your energy reserves have dropped drastically. You still find it increasingly difficult to stay focused.

As you watch the cloud float quietly across the afternoon sky, you pick up your newfound book from earlier in the day from off of your desk and search for possible answers. You find a chapter about courage and strength, exactly what you need to get through this stage of your long journey. The chapter, and the examples contained in it, talks about how warriors or excellent leaders have an excess of strength and energy that they use to get through difficult challenges and times. Warriors always have reserves of energy available to them, and never allow themselves to get burned out. They recognize the need to recharge those reserves when they sense they are running low.

With all of your strength and resolve, and using the newfound knowledge from your book, you slowly stand and stretch your aching back. Getting away from your home office, and out in the fresh air will be exactly what you need to recharge.

As you walk around your neighborhood, you follow the clouds as they move carelessly overhead. Just as the last cloud disappears from the sky, you reach your home again, feeling refreshed, even though you still have a long journey to the summit ahead of you.

The day is almost over as you wander back to your deck, exhausted from your day's adventures, but with a clear mind and a clearer sense of purpose. You are thankful; you made it through another day and you have learned the lesson of strength, a warrior's strength.

You will need that lesson more than ever when you continue your journey in the morning.

A Warrior's Checklist

Strength

We derive strength from many different sources in our personal and professional lives. Consider how you might use each of the following areas in your life to further develop your own personal strengths:

- Reflection and meditation
- Physical exercise
- Nutrition
- Motivation
- Goal setting

Goal-Setting

One of the most significant things that we sometimes lose in life are our routines. Those are good opportunities to think about our priorities and what is important to us in our everyday lives.

1. Identify one goal that you have for yourself, and that you can achieve in the short-term (one week or shorter).

2. Make note of one action that you can take every day that will help you to achieve the goal from the previous step. Note one obstacle that you may need to overcome in that

process, and the tools you might use to conquer that challenge.

3. Long term goals are also important because they give us something to look forward to every day when they are selected appropriately. Brainstorm at least two or three ideas for long term goals that you would like to accomplish.

4. Of those two or three goals, does one seem more attainable or of more importance to you? Make note of that goal.

5. Identify a handful of ways you can work toward that goal on a regular basis.

6. For that long-term goal, how will you know when you have met that goal? Be specific.

7. For that long-term goal, how will you maintain accountability to yourself to ensure that you continue to make progress toward that goal? Would it be helpful to keep a journal of your progress? Would it be motivational to share your goal with a close family member

or friend who will help you stick to your goal?

Phase 6:
Crucial Decisions

You have continued to struggle with your job search and are finding this to be one of the most difficult challenges you have ever faced in your professional life. In the course of the past week, your search has taken on a different and even greater sense of urgency. One of your best friends had recently been diagnosed with a terminal illness. While she had initially responded well to her treatments, her health took a sudden and dramatic turn for the worst a couple of days ago, and she passed away suddenly.

With her passing, you have come to question your priorities, your career, and your next steps in your own journey. You find yourself increasingly distracted and are have difficulty focusing on much of anything other than her death. It feels as though you are questioning and second-guessing everything.

Time and again, you find yourself returning to memories of your very first job many years ago. You worked in a small, local restaurant, and you absolutely loved the work, your co-workers and your customers. You find yourself longing for the creativity and pleasure that you took from that work. Cooking had been your passion from a very young age, but when you worked in the restaurant you were persuaded by family members to go in a different direction, to go to college, and to follow the path of business instead. For the most part, you have loved your career and value the skills that you have learned over the years, and the people that you have met. Perhaps not perfect, or even great, you are good at what you do. However, at this major time of transition in your life, you contemplate returning to the past to a job that was fulfilling, creative and fun, but that you had left behind many years ago to climb the corporate ladder.

Your friend's passing has caused you to seriously question the decisions that you have made in the course oyour career, and your life in general. You are facing a serious crisis of identity and are especially concerned that if you want to make a career change, that now is the time to do it. And if you don't, you fear that it will be too late.

But you also question your own motives in thinking about the past. Are you thinking about making a change for the right reasons? Are your memories of working in the restaurant authentic, or false, nostalgic memories of a time that you will never regain? Will your family be supportive of such a decision?

If you do make a change, will you be able to pay your mortgage and meet all of your other obligations? Life just isn't as simple as it once was—and decisions certainly not any easier.

The way ahead is dark, unknown, and full of stress and life-changing decisions. You struggle because you feel as though you have no one to speak with about your dilemma. There don't seem to be any easy or even obvious answers, and you're not sure how to begin thinking about such dramatic changes in your life.

§

Only a few short days ago, you thought your journey was almost over. Even now, you feel that the summit, a significant new opportunity, is near at hand. The economy has improved dramatically, you are getting callbacks from hiring managers, and you have even had a couple of interviews that went rather well. You anticipate your first new job offers to start in just a couple of short days, if everything continues to go well. This is the most progress you have made over the past couple of months, and you're feeling vastly better about the entire experience.

But in spite of the fact that the end of your job search seems to be near, you have started to have doubts.

In your mind, you hear the sound of past voices that represent others in your life that embarked upon their own professional adventures. Like you, many of them chose to climb the corporate ladder. And many have been professionally successful.

But you now begin to realize that something has been missing from your career and search. Even though you are finally achieving some success in the next stages of your journey, your heart just isn't in the search any longer. And that isn't helpful at all because you know that the next part of the journey will be one of the most difficult and require the most focus from you.

You turn inward for guidance, trusting that you will arrive

confidently and safely at your next destination.

Your challenge, though, is not an insignificant one: in trying to cope with the passing away of your friend and previous co-worker, you have come to feel that there is far more to life than such a relentless focus on your career.

You have taken stock of many things in your life as you have struggled with your job search, and you realize that you have missed out on a lot in your almost relentless focus. While you have focused on your career, you have missed family birthdays, worked through holidays, and passed up vacations. At the time, it always seemed like you were making the right decisions, focused on the path, but without taking the time to enjoy the journey and making note of where in life those decisions were taking you.

Even more than ever, it's probably fair to say that you have always been so busy that now you don't even really know how to relax any longer.

It has taken losing your job, and struggling to find a new path, to force you into the realization that there might be more to life that you have been missing all of these years. Your biggest fear is that it might be too late to make any changes for the better. You have a mortgage, car payments and other obligations that you don't think you can escape. In short, your relentless focus on your career has trapped you in a life without you fully realizing it until now. It has taken the passing away of your friend to force you to stop and take stock of where you find yourself in life and you aren't sure that you are very happy with where you currently find yourself.

If there is ever going be a way out from such an extremely toxic and dangerous trap, it is in the reality that warriors know that the path they seek is not just an external journey but an inner journey of self-awareness and a reprioritization of what is important in life.

Leadership involves having the internal wisdom and confidence to make the right decisions and to have the external experiences and resources that help to empower, uplift and encourage oneself to make the right decisions, even when they may lead you into the unknown and out of your comfort zone.

Under the right circumstances, those same life experiences and resources also have the potential to help others to be successful in their jobs and overall life as well. Warriors know that their journey is not theirs' alone but gains in power when shared with others.

Just as significantly, the best of leaders turns internally when it comes to significant, life-changing decisions. Leadership means having the courage and self-confidence to realize when you are on the wrong path, and to make the sometimes impossibly difficult seeming decision to take a new and different path—even if it means having to circle back on your path or start over in life. Courageous leaders know that sometimes one has to step backward in order to ultimately start moving forward again.

The critical question that you face right now, therefore, is one of timing: you have had the courage to take the first step on this part of your journey and acknowledge that you are most likely on the wrong path. But the real question you need to answer is whether or not you have progressed so far along the path that you can no longer turn back. It is time that you take a serious accounting of your journey and assess if you really are at a point of no return, or if there is still an opportunity to make some significant changes in your life.

You contemplate whether you should continue on your existing path in the corporate world to your next opportunity or return to your long-past passion where you feel as though you could incorporate your years of leadership skills and experience and open up your own café or restaurant. There's something to be said about being your own boss that seems appealing to you as well.

You acknowledge that you have enjoyed your leadership roles in the corporate world, even if the past few years have been stressful. Your decision feels like an impossibly difficult one. After a long day of worry and indecision, you eventually fall asleep knowing that warriors do not dwell long in indecision but use the tools of clarity and sense of purpose to seek direction and guidance.

Early the next morning, you recognize that you have no choice but to prepare for your metaphorical climb again if you are going to remain true to yourself: you still have some significant decisions to make.

You do not feel fully prepared for the steep journey that you face but you have to rely as best you can on what you have for resources. As always in life, we are not always ideally equipped or prepared for what life brings but we still have to make the most out of difficult or uncomfortable life circumstances and decisions. As a leader you will face insurmountable challenges day after day with employee conflicts, financial decisions, missed deadlines and company growth.

Sometimes the potentially positive challenges can be the most difficult to address. You recognize and honor the path of the warrior, as the path of leadership is not always an easy or direct one.

You take a deep breath and hold it for a moment as these decisions are not to be rushed or taken lightly. Perhaps a change of scenery will help.

With your life warrior book in hand, you mindfully walk a quiet path through a small park in your neighborhood and observe your surroundings. Unlike the easy path that you walk, the steps in your decision-making process look steep and difficult as the sides of the path around you plummet steeply. The risks ahead are significant and life altering.

You take another deep breath and summon the courage to move forward in your attempt to identify that ever-important first step or decision. As you feel yourself getting closer to making a decision, the similarities to climbing a steep path are even more striking to you. Perhaps because the decision also makes you anxious, your breathing becomes strained and your pulse quickens. You recognize the signs of anxiety and stress and remind yourself that every step in this process has to be mindful and considerate of your options. One false or careless move could cause you to slip and fall off the path and back to the beginning, plunging you back into darkness and a life of despair and a job or career that may no longer serve you. A step too far in the other direction could put you and your family at considerable risk, too.

If you leave the corporate world behind, you may regret it. On the other hand, if you follow a new, perhaps less known path, you may find happiness and a renewed sense of purpose in your life. This decision is the hardest you have ever made. There doesn't seem to be an easy way to choose the right path, let alone your next steps.

You struggle to breathe. You are exhausted by all of the challenges that you have faced, and by the rollercoaster of emotions that have resulted. Nothing seems easier than the hope that someone else will make this decision for you. But you know this must be your decision and that leaders need to be able to make impossible decisions without regret in the face of adversity.

With a growing sense of confidence in mind, you feel as though your need to make a decision picks up in intensity. You need to make it to the next phase in your journey. You also recognize that doubts still gather in your mind like dark, foreboding clouds. You recognize the old, familiar patterns of self-sabotage. You are able to stop those toxic thought patterns because you recognize that they are a normal part of the process. It isn't that warriors don't ever have feelings of doubt, but that they recognize them and proactively manage them by managing those things that are within their control—and learning to let go of that which they cannot control. Never is this as important as when the stakes are this high.

When the warrior makes a promise to lead, the universe conspires to test him or her and requires a regular recommitment to the journey, sometimes on a daily basis.

The warrior makes that commitment to move through moments of weakness, doubt or self-sabotage and uses new-found strength to continue moving forward because this is the way of the warrior, and there is no other way.

You continue your walk, and you also press on, toward a decision. You search out a place to rest both your body and your mind, even if momentarily, but you find nothing. You have no choice but to continue on.

The physical path is changing, the way beneath your feet slippery and wet. It reminds you of your decision: as never before in your journey, you recognize the need for mindfulness—a small misstep could send you spiraling into despair and loss.

You begin to question if you will make the right decision? You feel like each decision might require different leadership skills from you. In a new situation, will you be a good leader? Do you have what it takes?

Will you find personal fulfillment and satisfaction?

You stop briefly and turn back to see someone on the path behind you. They look worn out and as though they are struggling to continue on their path and personal journey. You begin to wonder if you are making your own journey just because the path beneath your feet is familiar to you. You wonder the same about the person you see behind you. You wonder if they have the same struggles as you.

Suspecting that you are unable to help them, you turn back to resume your walk. You take several more steps until you finally see a small wooden bench where you can stop for a short rest. Just as you reach the tiny spot along the side of the path, you recognize that perhaps you can help your fellow traveler behind you.

As you sit on the bench, you look at the book that you have been idly carrying with you this morning, and you recognize that it has fully served its purpose for you. If you leave it sitting on the bench, perhaps the person behind you will find it and benefit from it as well. Although your warrior's guide will be gone, you feel prepared to continue on your path alone.

Although you experience a moment of sadness, you know it is a temporary one. Warriors know that attachments to physical things is not healthy and always lead to suffering and loss. You also are fully aware that warriors and effective leaders know how to create new tools when they need them, for themselves as well as for others.

Although the book has been a helpful companion on your journey to this point, now it is time to pass it along to someone else who would benefit from its guidance.

With your book surrendered, you stand and look forward. You are thankful that you have made the right choice in helping someone else.

Further along the path, you turn briefly back and see the person stop at the small bench, find the book, pick it up and examine it. You imagine a look of interest and relief on his face. The book now becomes his companion on his journey, and you hope that he finds it useful. You smile. Although it was your loss, the book is his gain and perhaps much needed on his solo journey, wherever he is headed. You know that this warrior's tool will assist the man in his own professional adventures.

Warriors understand that the tools they find, and use are just temporary, and only become more powerful when they are shared with others or are used when leading teams.

This morning's walk has been challenging and difficult in the sense that you have learned to let go as part of your decision-making process. In your surrender of the familiar, however, you have learned that in the process of creating your own tools and inner strength, that you are well on your way to the final stop in this leg of your journey: a decision about your next path in life. However, you also feel isolated and alone in the sense that few have made it this far in their own journeys. It looks as though you will have to spend the rest of your journey alone–even if you are not far from your goal: either the pinnacle of your career or a brand-new adventure.

You reflect on the morning's lessons.

The past no longer grips you in fear and doubt as it has before, but concern about how your life and career will change remain on the surface of your mind. You recognize that purely from fear, you have clung to nostalgic memories of the past that may no longer have a basis in reality. While you recognize that your path might not be precisely the one that you thought you set forth on, you also know that dwelling in the past is counterproductive.

You choose to stop those thoughts for now, not yet concerned about tomorrow as you focus on the present moment and on how far you have come on your journey. All will be well. You have made it further in your journeys than most. As a warrior and a leader, you have conquered many obstacles and assembled powerful tools. All that you have learned, all that you have experienced will not only help you to make the right decision, but to also lead others as you strive to become the best warrior and leader possible. With that thought firmly in mind, the ultimate path that you take seems less significant to you, and you take great comfort in that knowledge.

Later that night, as you begin to drift off to sleep, you find a regained confidence in the solace of your journey. Perhaps there is no wrong path at this point in your journey, provided that you choose your direction for the right reasons.

§

Sometime in the middle of the night, you awake abruptly as the ground beneath your bed seems to rumble and move in the darkness. You don't know what is happening, if you are even awake, but you are terrified. Have you climbed all of this way, only to crash and fall? Is this all really happening, or are you still dreaming?

Fleetingly, you feel the irrational desire to run. You have no set direction in mind and the four walls surrounding you sway from side to side. It feels as though you are experiencing an earthquake of great magnitude.

You don't know what to do. It feels as though everything is gone. Rather than run, you huddle in place for the rest of the night until the movement stops and everything feels as though it has settled back into place. You stay put, not sleeping, until the morning sun rises.

Stiff and exhausted, you stand, stretch and know that you are alone, and it feels as though nothing remains in life. What little you had is gone. You have finally completely and fully entered the world of the warrior. You recognize this moment as the time where you must ultimately step into the role of authentic leadership.

A Warrior's Checklist

Personal Attachments

Ask yourself these questions about personal attachments in your life:

- What or who are you attached to?
- How does the attachment serve you?
- How does the attachment cause you pain or suffering?
- Is the attachment healthy?
- Does the attachment serve your higher good or higher purpose?
- If necessary, how can you let go of the attachment?

Path

1. Sometimes, we also get attached to the journeys that we believe we are on. In a sentence describe your own journey.

2. How have you become attached to that journey?

3. If you could choose to make a change to that path, what one change would you make?

4. How would the change in your path, alter your journey? Describe one positive change. Describe one fear or concern that you have about making that change.

Phase 7:
The Professional Warrior's Summit

It is a time of significant change in your life. An opportunity recently surfaced with a relatively new company in the area. They would like you to join their team in a key leadership role. It would mean a significant raise and a promotion over the position that you lost many months ago. You have been told that you need to make a decision and they would like you to start very soon.

You are excited by the opportunity, but there's just one catch: you're fairly certain the position comes with significant personal and professional risk. Do you play it safe, and continue your search?

Or do you take a chance with the new startup, change paths and begin your adventure anew? What if the change ends your career?

What if the company isn't successful?

What if you aren't up to the challenges of a new position?

You'd like to make a decision quickly, but it feels like you have more questions than answers.

§

Your last stage of the journey lies ahead of you, and it will take every ounce of mental and physical strength you have if you are to navigate the decisions that you need to make. You have spent considerable time thinking about new career opportunities. But this one is different because it comes with significant professional risk to you, and you hadn't anticipated that being part of your decision. On top of that, you had also been thinking about stepping outside of your career and comfort zone and pursuing past passions instead. You have options, but the way forward is suddenly less clear than it had been.

You think about the opportunity with the new company, feeling as though you have nothing but the clothes on your back and nothing around you that will assist you in this stage of your journey. Somehow you need to make a decision.

It doesn't help that the job offer was a little unexpected, and that they are requesting that you make a decision relatively quickly.

You know that you will have to call upon every bit of your warriors' strength and courage if you are to make the right decision and move forward.

You start off on the remaining leg of the most difficult journey of your lifetime with mostly thoughts of courage and strength as you take your initial steps back onto the strenuous path toward your decision.

Although you have nothing with you materially, you recognize that you are emotionally, mentally, and physically equipped to choose your next path in your career. With these abilities, you know that you have to summon every ounce of courage for these final next steps. With a newfound sense of purpose, you resolutely set off.

In your head, the path before you gains quickly in elevation, representing the significance of your next steps. But you also feel as though you are breathing and thinking stronger and clearer than you have in months. You are mindful of the dangerous pitfalls around you, but you don't let those hinder you in any way.

You can now see all that you have left behind, far in the past;

you are no longer pulled by the energy of things left behind, your old career, stability, routines.

Relying instead on new, healthy habits and ways of seeing the world around you, you know that if you are to make a decision about a new job, you need to keep your head clear and focused on a way forward.

This morning you set off on a new and different path, alone and without your running group, and without morning coffee afterward. Instead you choose a quiet walk in the woods intentionally alone, yet mindful of the decisions that you will need to make, even if you are uncertain precisely how you will make them. Halfway along the trail, you spot an Ipod in the middle of the trail that was left behind by another warrior. You feel as though someone has abandoned their journey, retreating back to their past, leaving a trail of unwanted items, and returning to a previous career and an old lifestyle.

Without thinking too much about it, you slip the Ipod and ear buds in your pocket, knowing that you will put them to good use. You are reminded that warriors are often taken care of in unexpected ways and that the outside world provides them with everything they need, each and every step of their journey.

This morning, however, your mind races with the decision that you have to make, and each and every step still feels like a thousand steps as you try and remain focused. After struggling with your walk for what feels like a lifetime, you are exhausted, and you begin to think that you can't go on. You knew the journey would be difficult but didn't know it was going to be this hard. You are uncertain of the path to choose in order to move forward.

You have thoughts of self-doubt, and about giving up but then you remember the Ipod in your pocket. You turn it on, and an inspirational lock screen message appears that says simply,

"Courage". You keep walking trying to turn your thoughts back to the new opportunity with the small startup company and the decision that you face.

You feel less tempted by the option of turning back. The warrior's way is always forward.

You know that life brings challenges and unexpected opportunities to test your strength and courage. This is one of those tests, and you resolve not to give in to past fears. You swallow your fear and begin to look for a way of thinking about your current decision, knowing that choosing instead to wait for a safe but dead-end job will surely result in the death of your spirit and career, and a life of regret. Warriors know that there is more to satisfying and successful careers that can be lost if one is overly concerned about always making what feel like safe choices.

While the startup company may carry significant risks if you accept the position, you have come to realize that those things in life that are most worthwhile do often carry risk with them. As a warrior, you understand that it is better to risk and to lose, than to not make a valiant effort. You do not want your life to be one of regrets at opportunities not taken.

With strident step, you continue walking and your confidence grows slowly but surely. The process is painfully hard, your progress labored, but you remain resolute. Although you are on nothing more than a simple gravel walking path, the stress of your decision makes you feel as though you are on a grueling and steep hike. As with many of life's most difficult decisions, there is nothing to prevent you from failing. One misstep in your decision-making process could well result in a deadly fall. You focus single mindedly on each footstep and the final decision ahead.

Great leaders and warriors are tested beyond the bounds of mere mortals. You have made the journey this far and you know there is no turning back. As a warrior, you pull yourself out of this momentary weakness, confident in the strength you have gained along the way. When you make the decision to become whole, nothing will prevent you from fulfilling your mission to becoming your authentic self, no matter how hard, or difficult the path or obstacles that lie ahead.

With clarity of mind, and a renewed strength, you push onward and upward. You still cannot see the ultimate step in your journey, but you know it is there and you know that you are getting closer. After years of climbing and spending time in dead-end jobs, you are as close as you can be to achieving your goals.

You round a gentle curve in the path, and with one final step, and with conviction, you suddenly find yourself standing on top of the summit. You have arrived.

A Warrior's Checklist

Personal Power

We often overlook the role that personal control plays or could play in our own lives. Consider the possibilities of the following questions:

1. Where in your life do you exhibit control over your own decisions that works particularly well for you?

2. Identify at least one area in life that feels as though it is out of your control. What might

you do in order to regain some control by focusing on aspects of the situation that you might influence?

3. When you look to the lives of others, what do you see them controlling, in a constructive fashion?

4. Identify one approach that you think might work in your own personal situation.

The Professional Pinnacle

After what seems a lifetime, you suddenly find yourself standing at the top of your professional summit.

You have no thoughts, no words to describe the view from your destination. The summit holds a power, or energy that you have been searching for, for an entire lifetime. The vistas are astonishingly beautiful, arrayed in rich oranges and reds.

For a brief moment, you stop and reflect on your journey and your surroundings. The self-doubt, seemingly impossible decisions, difficult co-workers and all of the other obstacles that you have faced to get to this point come into sharp focus for you. You have passed all of these tests, and the journey has been worthwhile. And you are grateful to everyone who aided you along your way.

Even as you have accomplished much in this journey, you look up from your path, and outward to the horizon. From this vantage point, you see many mountains, many summits in your future that you didn't realize were there for you until you finally had the courage to step out of your comfort zone. Rather than a sense of fear and foreboding, the multiple peaks fill you with a sense of awe, adventure, and wonder.

You recognize a new truth that every day you will have other summits to climb. Each will be unique, and you will arrive at each of them in new, challenging, and wondrous ways. Rather than fear the unknown, you embrace the challenges that you know will be thrown at you by different situations. You recognize that sometimes you will be forced back down into dangerous valleys and canyons before once again attaining another summit. Successes are but small, fleeting victories on your journey ever higher to learning about your inner warrior.

Over time, you know you will climb not only for yourself but also for and with your team members and colleagues. Every climb will be different, requiring vigilance and continued focus. Each will have their own unique challenges and dangers, though the warrior will find that each will become easier as the load you carry with you will lighten with every trip. The warrior's tools will also change and evolve with every journey, becoming useful in different and more relevant ways when you most need them, but only if you are mindful and care for those tools.

You have learned how to navigate the challenges you have faced, but remain mindful that the world never stays the same and your journey will also evolve and change.

After your long journey, you can envision a royal blue banner waving strong and proud at your personal summit. The banner represents the ending of this leg of your adventure, but also the beginning of new journeys. You know that others will make similar professional pilgrimages, and you understand that they may benefit if you share your experiences with them.

The banner serves as a symbolic reminder of your journey for others who may follow your path.

Physically alone for this brief moment in time, you come to recognize that you, too, have benefited from the many others who have made their own journeys before you.

The morning sun shines through the soft boughs of the pine trees surrounding the gravel travel that you stand upon. You feel an overwhelming sense of relief from leaving behind a career that did not motivate you or provide you with the tools or skills that you so wanted and needed to have. Ultimately, it matters not if it was by choice, or otherwise.

Similar issues or problems both personally and professionally will arise in your future, but now you are equipped to address those challenges head on as a warrior and authentic leader.

You sit briefly in a suspended moment of silence on the summit, unsure of exactly what lies ahead of you. You might feel the desire to stay on top of the summit forever, but you have to leave soon—such places were never intended as final destinations but only as stopping places to serve a temporary need along the way in a longer journey that lies ahead of you. Perhaps the transient nature of the summit is part of its elusive allure as your purpose now will also be to teach others to take your place someday.

Warriors find, create, and build new paths. You recognize that building paths for others to follow will now be a part of your life's work. As you create those new paths, you will also create maps with words, pictures and experiences to share with others who also desire to make similar journeys in their lives.

Just as you give thanks to the mountain summit for its beautiful yet harsh lessons, you see something glistening on the ground beneath you. You pick up the shining, golden key. It looks old but the metal end of the key is wrought into a familiar shape.

It is an image of the three interlocking triangles, the same image that you saw carved in the cement floor in your office at the beginning of your journey. It is a symbol of wholeness, representing strength, endurance and achievement.

You hold the golden key in the palm of your hand understanding somehow that it was placed there for you to find at this moment in your ongoing journey. It is a tangible reminder that you have succeeded in climbing to the summit; you have overcome multiple adversities and now you have the strength to make the personal journey to new summits day after day.

You are the warrior. You will continue to succeed in your climb to the everyday summit personally and professionally, no matter what life's adversities bring: climb, conquer and succeed.

A Warrior's Checklist

Use this list as a reminder of the lessons learned from the phases in your journey along your way to the summit:

Commitment to Change

A Path of Transformation

Navigating Treacherous Water

Professional Darkness

Climbing Higher

Crucial Decisions

The Professional Summit

The Professional Pinnacle

1. In your career, you have most certainly been aided or influenced by many others around you. Choose one of those individuals. Make note of how they have influenced you. List one tangible way you feel gratitude toward that individual. If it feels appropriate, share your gratitude directly with that individual.

2. With the same individual in mind, think about someone else in your life who is currently struggling with their own journey. How can you help influence their journey in a positive way?

THE END

Appendices

Our work and professions provide us with seemingly endless challenges and opportunities. Although we cannot capture all of them here, nor can we necessarily provide direct answers, we do have additional scenarios that you might find helpful as you reflect upon and have to choose how to respond to your own professional challenges as a warrior.

Scenarios

1. *After years of toiling in your current position, you have finally been recognized for your contributions to your organization and offered a new opportunity. Your boss has been extremely supportive of your move but has asked if you will be willing to continue helping out your current*

department for a few weeks as they hire your replacement.

2. During your annual reviews, you've been consistently told that you are one of the department's–and company's–top performers! That's music to your ears, but you still regularly and consistently get passed over for new opportunities and promotion. Unexpectedly, your supervisor gives you a huge break. The only dilemma: it requires that you travel to Europe for two weeks to temporarily help out a satellite office that is short-staffed and facing tight deadlines for a significant merger with another company. You're excited about the opportunity, but there's only one problem: you have family obligations and cannot be away from home for two weeks. You're faced with a classic dilemma: do you choose family or career?

3. As part of a very small team, you have played a central role in delivering a crucial new service to your organization. There's just one tiny little problem: your boss has taken all of the credit for the success of the project.

4. You just returned from your company's annual meeting where you learned that

it was an even more difficult year for sales than the company was projecting. Next year doesn't look much better. You're stressed out, to put it mildly: you've invested a significant number of years in this company and your career here, and you're no more than a handful of years away from retirement. The company has already announced that they will be offering a combination of early retirements and buy-outs to try and manage the financial crisis they find themselves facing. You've always wanted an opportunity to try a business venture of your own, and this might be your chance. But you'll be potentially risking a significant portion of your retirement, as well as financial support for health insurance. It's far from an easy solution as both paths could carry significant risk or reward.

5. *Over the past 12 months or so, you've been struggling at work. You and your supervisor aren't communicating well, your projects are languishing and–quite frankly–you're not feeling very valued by your organization. You've been looking for an opportunity elsewhere for quite some time and have been frustrated by the lack of interest by other employers. So, it comes as a surprise when one of your company's key competitors offers you a*

position with them. To say that you are eager to leave your current company and position is an understatement at best. The opportunity comes with a new promotion and a raise. Although you can't quite pinpoint the exact concern, something doesn't feel right about the position. Do you try and remain patient in your current position, hoping that you find something better—or that your fortune turns in your current position? Or do you risk it, and get out of what might best be described as a losing situation?

6. You have been working in your organization for over 24 years and feel as though you have never been recognized for your skills or dedication. You can leave the organization and risk losing benefits, perhaps taking a lesser position, or remain stuck in your current position until retirement. The decision has been weighing so heavily on your mind that you have started seeking counseling for depression.

7. You have been ordered by your employer to attend counseling for drug and alcohol abuse. You blame a combination of a stressful job and difficult home situation and are reluctant to attend.

8. *A combination of stresses from what you consider to be a toxic work environment have started to make you physically ill, and you feel increasingly unable to fulfill the duties of your position. Worse, your family has also noticed the emotional and physical toll the job is taking on you and those around you. They are pressuring you almost daily to make changes.*

9. *For the past several months, you have been eagerly developing a number of new programs and products for your employer. You find the work richly rewarding, and you have never felt as valued as an employee. Unexpected changes outside of the control of you or your employer suddenly change all of that and you find yourself out of work, and adrift without the purpose of the programs you were developing.*

10. *After years of hard work and commitment, you have been promoted into a position that you thought would be your dream job. But shortly after starting, you discover that it is anything but your dream: the money is great, and the work isn't terrible. But your heart isn't in it, you're becoming increasingly stressed out and would like to leave, but you feel*

trapped by the position, and everything that comes with it. You also worry about how your family members and friends will feel if you walk away from something that you had always dreamed of for yourself.

11. *When you started your current position, it was with the expectation that when you finished your college education, you would be promoted into a fulltime, permanent position more to your suiting. However, you have been since passed over multiple times, and feel like you're stuck in a rut. You are concerned that your colleagues will always see you in your current role and not give you the opportunities that you feel you have earned.*

Copyright © 2020 Tomorrow River Publishing

All rights reserved. This book or any portion thereof may not be reproduced or used in any manner whatsoever without the express written permission of the publisher except for the use of brief quotations in a book review.

Printed in the United States of America.

First Edition
First printing, October 2020

Tomorrow River Publishing
1017 Lindbergh Avenue
Stevens Point, WI 54481

www.tomorrowriverpublishing.com

TOMORROW RIVER GAMES

ISBN: 9798670363389

Made in the USA
Las Vegas, NV
06 September 2022